THE BUTTERFLY IMPACT

THE BUTTERFLY
IMPACT

Resilience, Resets,
and Ripples

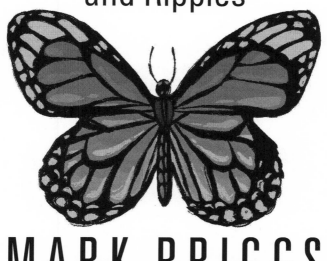

MARK BRIGGS

HOUNDSTOOTH
PRESS

THE BUTTERFLY IMPACT
Resilience, Resets, and Ripples

ISBN   978-1-5445-2441-2 *Hardcover*
       978-1-5445-2439-9 *Paperback*
       978-1-5445-2440-5 *Ebook*

To my sons, Sam and Giallo

May you find your own path and purpose,
filled with resilience and ripples.

I can't wait to see the Impact you make on our world.

CONTENTS

PART 3: WELCOME TO THE FUTURE

ABOUT THIS BOOK

A quick note about the structure and format of this book: I spoke with dozens of colleagues, experts, and friends while writing *The Butterfly Impact* and combined those conversations and insights with other research from books, articles, podcasts, and videos. If I spoke directly with a source, I refer to that person by their first name. If I'm quoting from an external source, I refer to that person by their last name.

The Introduction is meant to explain the concept of The Butterfly Impact and set up the rest of the book. Each chapter describes a pillar in the foundation of my concept of The Butterfly Impact.

Each of the subsequent chapters includes a BUTTERFLY IMPACT SIGNPOST to signify the key takeaway from that chapter, and actionable recommendations under the MAKING IT HAPPEN subhead. I hope these elements help you make the most of the lessons included in the book.

Part 1 describes various methods of and approaches to doing work differently, disrupting the status quo and finding nonobvious solutions to common problems. Part 2 addresses work as a team sport, because the ability to interact with other people is not only required in most jobs, but those interactions and relationships can often make or break your experience.

Part 3, the final stop on this journey, views The Butterfly Impact through the lens of 2020. It will help you think about how to apply the lessons from previous chapters in this era of unprecedented uncertainty, to make the most of your resets and create impactful ripples throughout your world.

PROLOGUE

HAPPINESS IS AN ACCOMPLISHMENT

How I came to be a student of personal growth, positive thinking, resilience, and happiness is a bit of a horror show, honestly. Two failed marriages and family turmoil forced me to navigate through some serious shit.

My early life went much better. I grew up in an idyllic Idaho lake town with a solid, loving family, surrounded by a large group of close friends and constant adventure—a storybook come to life. I took it for granted and assumed that most people had this foundation.

I went to college at Gonzaga University in Spokane, Washington, with a plan to become a high school football coach. Both of my older sisters were in school there, and I had cousins, aunts, and uncles who were Zag alumni, too. It was a family thing and, if I learned nothing else from my parents, I learned to cherish family at an early age.

My introduction to journalism came during my sophomore year. I had a weekly assignment to write a news article that would be passed on to the college newspaper editors for review, and they published the first article I submitted. Once I saw my byline in the school paper, I was hooked. After graduation I started working as a sportswriter for local newspapers, combining my passion for sports and journalism. Writing came easily, and watching sports while getting paid (very little) felt like a no-brainer.

A couple years later, I was bored. Covering sports felt like the movie *Groundhog Day*. Everything had a set schedule, a defined cadence. Football followed baseball, basketball followed football, and so on. One summer night, sitting by the campfire at my family's lake cabin with my first wife, we thought up a new plan: quit our jobs and move across the country so I could attend graduate school and get a master's degree. Part of me still wanted to coach, and I thought teaching in college seemed like a sensible alternative and a fulfilling professional future.

After completing my master's degree at the University of North Carolina in Chapel Hill, we moved back to the Pacific Northwest. I started working for newspapers again, this time on the digital side and in management. Eventually I started writing books about digital journalism at the suggestion of a respected colleague.

At the time, new technologies and new internet platforms exploded into our lives. I developed an insatiable entrepreneurial itch as I tried to help newspapers transition into this digital age. Eventually I quit my job to launch a startup company in 2008, right into the teeth of the global recession. Despite the timing, it seemed like we had a safe plan to manage our family finances, which included budgeting to send our two young children to Catholic school. My wife had a full-time job and benefits, our safety net. But the following year, she got laid off. We had to meet with the principal of the kids' school to ask for financial help. My startup company struggled as the customer base reeled from the recession. I managed to earn enough money with speaking gigs and consulting work, thanks to my books. This work meant that I traveled often. Still, my wife and I were both consumed by the stress of not knowing how we would pay the mortgage in a few months.

Then, things went totally off the rails. I discovered my wife was having an affair. My work travel, while keeping us financially afloat, was taking me away from the marriage when she needed me home. She had also stopped paying the mortgage and other bills, while running up massive credit card debt—and I had no idea any of this was happening. We went through three different marriage counselors, and I started seeing my own therapist. We tried everything we could to save the marriage, but nothing worked. I had never been to any counseling and grew up associating therapy with weakness, thanks to the culture around me. Over time, I began to see the benefits of therapy and counseling.

I spent the next few years sorting through my own guilt, anger, depression, and anxiety over the impact this would have on our kids. The shame of failing at the one thing I knew I wanted to do with my life—build the kind of family I grew up in—haunted me. The requirements of a job can't be separated from the demands of a family, and I failed to balance the two. They are at odds but totally dependent on each other.

It took more counseling (and lots of books) plus countless, deep, soul-searching conversations with close friends and my sister to sort through the guilt, anger, depression, and anxiety.

My mantra during this time, "just keep doing the right thing," helped me focus on being the best dad I could be. I didn't want my kids to feel like they were growing up in a "broken family."

A few years later, I started dating a woman whom I had known professionally for a couple years. She lit up my world in a way I didn't know was possible. I had never been so close to someone as dynamic, inspiring, loving, and fun. Everything in our relationship happened fast. We were engaged in six months and married within a year. I knew she battled anxiety and depression, but I was confident I could "save" her. She worked harder at managing life than anyone I'd ever met. She had no choice. She had to work ten times harder than most people do just to be a normally operating person in the world. I learned so much from her about how to be a better person—and a better partner—but it turned out to not be enough.

When I asked her to marry me under the Bean, a sculpture in Chicago's Millennium Park, it felt like I was living in a movie. We frequently shared the deepest talks of my life and, when the energy between us flowed in the right direction, I struggled for words to describe the feeling. I told friends it must be like winning the Super Bowl as a football player: realizing your dreams coming true right in front of you.

But our dream-come-true became a nightmare. Once we moved in together everything quickly fell apart. Her anxiety and depression got worse and worse. The rollercoaster ride that once had ups and downs became a constant downward spiral into chaos, hurt, anguish, and fear. She became physically abusive; I routinely had scratches and bruises on my body. I locked myself in the bathroom a few times to escape. The police intervened—twice. She was suicidal. Once I tackled her in our bedroom to wrestle a knife out of her hands as she threatened to use it on herself.

We tried counseling—hours and hours of counseling. I read more books, and had more soul-searching conversations with friends and family. I learned everything I could about abusive and dysfunctional relationships—how to fix them and, eventually, how to end them.

I was deeply concerned about my kids and the toll this marriage was taking on them—and on our relationship. I had shared custody fifty-fifty with their mom since our divorce, but eventually the kids asked to stay at their mom's house full time. I couldn't bear the thought of losing my kids. On a sunny spring day, confident that I had done everything in my power to make it work, I walked away from my second marriage.

As my kids and I adjusted to our new, more peaceful life, my younger child confided in me (and his mom and brother) that he thought he was born the wrong gender. He wanted to start exploring a female-to-male gender transition. (He attended a Catholic school where the uniform required girls to wear a plaid jumper, only one of many new challenges we had to navigate.) I had never met a transgender person, and had no idea what it meant to have gender dysphoria or what a transition entailed.

Enter: more counseling, more books, more deep soul-searching conversations with friends and family.

And this time I had a new job to get the hang of, too.

I had just accepted a job as a consultant with a firm out of Los Angeles. Before that, I had been working at a TV station in Seattle for seven years, enduring a brutal commute from my house in Tacoma. I had spent almost three hours each day driving, catching the train and walking to the office. In my new role, I worked from home but traveled frequently. I quickly discovered I loved working from home and traveling every couple of weeks to visit places like New York, San Francisco, Chicago, and Los Angeles. The relief from the daily commute and the excitement of a new opportunity couldn't have come at a better time.

* * *

My job gives me the chance to work with people at all levels, from the bosses and corporate presidents to the front-line staff. The challenges we are facing together—leading companies through massive disruption and trying to stay relevant to ever-changing audiences—has given me the perfect lab to test ideas on what a modern, adaptive culture should be. There's no road map, though. I'm inventing my job on the fly every day.

Luckily, I have plenty of support, from books and through conversations with smart, innovative friends and colleagues—and anyone else who will help me.

I also went back to school. As I had set out to do all those years ago, I began teaching in college. As luck would have it, the opportunity came from the University of North Carolina, where I had attended graduate school. I teach an master's level course online course each spring. It focuses heavily on change management and leading innovation for organizations. The students are mid-career professionals with full-time jobs and families, so work-life balance is a constant theme. I feel I've learned more from my students than they have from me, for which I'm grateful.

Having faced extremely challenging personal situations and a mix of incredible professional opportunities, I've had to learn, try, learn, try again and then learn some more. Work and life are what we do, but *how* we do it makes all the difference.

I started writing this book in 2019 but didn't get very far. I had some vague ideas on how I could help the people I saw trying to love their jobs, and their lives, while being overwhelmed by stress, burnout, and the demands of daily life. I couldn't pinpoint a way to bring all my ideas together at the time. Then the pandemic changed everything. Suddenly I found myself writing short essays and recommendations for my clients, as well as researching and thinking of ideas to help them manage through the crisis and lead their teams. Those writings began to spill over into what I had already considered for this book project. Then it all melded, and I found a sense of purpose that had been missing.

We will look back on 2020 as the year that changed the conventional structure of work forever. The global pandemic forced the world's workforce into a more collaborative and more meaningful state of work, one supportive of a more fulfilling life. This book is my attempt to offer a useful set of lessons and tactics that you can easily implement to better your life, both personally and professionally.

As someone who has learned to adapt to one challenge after another, I strongly believe that a new path to personal balance, productivity, and fulfillment will cause a ripple effect through our lives. It means becoming more valuable to our organizations, communities and culture while enjoying our own lives even more. I call this new approach The Butterfly Impact. I am honored to have you join me on this journey.

INTRODUCTION

THE BUTTERFLY EFFECT VS.
THE BUTTERFLY IMPACT

Little things can cause big changes—in work, in your personal life and, every so often, in both at the same time. This is the essence of The Butterfly Impact and the premise of this book: prioritizing your work-life happiness by making small changes will lead to more meaningful living and reverberate throughout your world.

To illustrate this, let's go back to the year 2000. My first wife and I had just moved back to the Pacific Northwest from North Carolina after I finished graduate school and she was pregnant with our first child. I had taken a new job running the website of a local newspaper in Everett, Washington, just north of Seattle. My title was "new media editor" since, at the time, everything digital was new. At the time, everything else in my life was new, too.

One day, I was in a meeting to brainstorm new ideas for a

potential grant project aimed at finding innovative ways to involve regular people in a community process. Since we were competing with other news organizations around the nation for this grant money, the more innovative, the better. We were focusing on four undeveloped waterfront areas around Everett, Washington, which the city and county wanted to use. However, they were undecided about the best way to use the land. More importantly to those of us at the newspaper, what did the tax-paying citizens want the city and county to do with the land? In researching other waterfront redevelopment efforts, we heard about an example from Vancouver, Washington, in which local citizens were invited to a public meeting and asked to draw their ideas for a new riverfront development on big flip charts of white paper with Sharpie pens.

"We should do that—but on our website," I suggested, even though I had no clue how my idea would actually work.

Fast forward the story: we developed the idea, won the grant to help fund the software programming to make it happen and partnered with an interactive firm out of Seattle to actually build it. Using the Flash programming framework, our technology partners helped us develop one of the world's first interactive clickable maps online—four years *before* Google Maps was born.

Thousands of people used the online tool to vote for their waterfront ideas, and local officials developed the areas with guidance from our online collaborative maps. People were able to click and drag icons representing parks or shopping and place them on the map where they wished they would go. *I have to admit, it was pretty cool.*

The resulting synchronicity changed my life. I won an innovation award from the Pew Center for Civic Journalism, the nonprofit that had given us the grant, and traveled to the University of North Carolina to receive it. That weekend I met the nonprofit's Executive Director, Jan Schaffer. During the process, I also met Glenn Thomas, who was running the interactive firm in Seattle that built out the software project. He would become the co-founder of my first startup company and someone I continue collaborating with today.

A few years later, I saw that Jan was traveling to Seattle to speak at a conference of newspaper editors, so I emailed her to invite her to meet for lunch. By then I had moved to Tacoma and was leading digital efforts for the newspaper there. I had created training classes to teach the newspaper's editors and reporters how to use audio, video, and blogging to keep pace with the changing technologies and audiences. It was clear that without more digital adoption, newspapers were heading for a downfall. Although the classes were optional, most were packed. People were hungry to learn. I remember joking with the executive editor, David Zeeck, that I was getting a better turnout than his mandatory staff meetings.

Over lunch, I told Jan this story and she simply replied, "You should write a book."

While I had occasionally daydreamed about writing the great American novel, I had never considered writing a non-fiction book—much less one about digital journalism. It seemed impractical to write a book about technology and tools that seemed to be changing every day. *It also sounded like a lot of work!*

Jan found grant funding for the project to compensate me for the time it would take to write the book. It wasn't much money, but with two young kids in Catholic school and a mortgage to pay, every little bit helped. Plus, something about the opportunity captivated me. I felt drawn to how much I would have to learn in order to create something that helped others understand all the different tactics and tools that were constantly emerging. This is why I call myself an accidental author. My first book, *Journalism 2.0: How to Survive and Thrive in the Digital Age*, was published in 2007 and translated into five languages. The Knight Foundation, thanks to the grant that Jan had secured, also offered it as a free PDF that was downloaded more than 200,000 times.

The idea about the crowdsourced waterfront development map had little apparent impact on my life at the time. Looking back, I realize that it sent my life in a new direction. This phenomenon is called the butterfly effect. It is perhaps most famously described by Jeff Goldblum's character in the film *Jurassic Park*: "a butterfly can flap its wings in Peking, and in Central Park, you get rain instead of sunshine." It is considered a part of chaos theory, in which Edward Lorenz (among others) combined the disciplines of meteorology and math. The central idea is that very small changes in a system can result in big changes downstream after a while.

"In popular culture, the term 'butterfly effect' is almost always misused," General Stanley McChrystal writes in *Team of Teams*. "It has become synonymous with 'leverage'—the idea of a small thing that has a big impact, with the implication that, like a lever, it can be manipulated to a desired end. This misses the point of Lorenz's insight. The reality is that small things in a complex system may have no effect or a massive one, and it is virtually impossible to know which will turn out to be the case."

BUTTERFLY IMPACT SIGNPOST

The butterfly *effect*, which has been studied for decades, shows us that we cannot predict the future, nor can we guide it. The best we can hope for is a holistic view of how small changes can lead to big impacts. Think of it as a lens, not a lever.

The Butterfly Impact, on the other hand, is my own hypothesis. By making small changes for immediate, personal benefit you will, over time, cause a ripple effect of compounded positive outcomes. This is very much a lever, but you should think of it as a series of very small levers instead of just one big one.

The lessons and real-life examples in this book are meant to illustrate this power that you possess. Let me give you a clear and simple perspective on how it has worked in my life.

Following the publication of *Journalism 2.0* in 2007, I went on to write *Journalism Next* (now in its fourth edition) and *Entrepreneurial Journalism*, both of which are widely used in college classrooms. While writing journalism textbooks does not bring fame and riches, those books led to speaking opportunities around the United States and in places like Denmark, Dubai, and China. I met incredible people at every stop. Those experiences also helped me learn what truly inspires me professionally and where I could make the biggest impact: helping others learn and grow. I figured out how to connect my passion for work with my passion for life, thanks to the challenges that you read about in the Prologue.

That first idea for the Everett waterfront project back in 2001 was a small lever that I pulled to make a positive change at the newspaper where I was working at the time. It has reverberated throughout my world—and impacted many others—and will continue to do so for decades to come. I continue to receive emails from journalists, professors and students in seemingly random parts of the world I've barely heard of, almost fifteen years after *Journalism 2.0* came to life.

Recognizing potential changes that you can make, however small, is much different than thinking you can cause big changes or produce some large-scale effect. Those small changes may lead to something bigger, but that's not necessarily the reason to make them.

Finding work-life happiness has always been a challenge, but now, as we emerge from the COVID pandemic, it demands large measures of resilience, hope, and an appreciation for the few silver linings to be found in 2020. Well-being at work also demands a new way of thinking about *how* we work, and the place that work has in our lives.

90,000 HOURS AND WHAT DO YOU GET?

The way most of us work is based on the factory system that started in the late eighteenth century during the Industrial Revolution. Today only a small fraction of US workers report being highly engaged in their work. That's a problem, since most will spend upwards of 90,000 hours at work during their lifetime.[1]

Yes, roughly one-third of your time on this planet will be at work. Depressing, isn't it?

What if we changed the way we approached work? What if we

leveraged the opportunities available to us in a modern, connected world to find more fulfillment? What if we could create a more rewarding return on the time and effort spent while on the job?

"When we teach people how to be leaders, 95 percent of the feedback is how the leadership model affects their family," says Bob Chapman, CEO of Barry-Wehmiller, a $2 billion manufacturing company with 12,000 employees around the world.[2] Chapman has pioneered a radical approach to running a company; it's based on people caring for one another. *Crazy, I know.* It has not only been good for business—it's been life-changing for his employees.

"I didn't realize that when we set that goal of sending people home fulfilled that they would, in turn, treat those around them the way they were being treated," says Chapman. "We found that caring is contagious. It was astounding to me, we realized in this journey, the way we treat people at work profoundly affects the way they go home and treat people in their span of care."

Chapmen says that people don't feel safe at work; instead, they feel used for someone else's success.

"We are clearly self-destructing as a society in chasing of economic value, which we assume is happiness, and, beyond a level of subsistence, there is no relationship between money and happiness."

The old-fashioned way of thinking, of course, is that you get paid for work, so what's all this nonsense about happiness? It's called work, after all, and the reward comes every two weeks on payday. Too often people think that if you want more work-life happiness, you simply need a job that pays more money—or grind for a promotion to middle management and a higher salary. The stories and examples to come offer a different view.

YOUR PLACE AND YOUR PURPOSE

Kimmie Sakamoto Timoney has always loved writing. She contributed to her high school newspaper and, after a couple years at Fresno City College, she earned a degree in broadcast journalism from San Francisco State. She loved that, as a journalist, she could provide local citizens and readers with important information and news. After an internship at a TV station, she was hired full time to write and publish online news articles as a web producer. Her news judgment, hard work and hustle have led to one promotion after another.

Ten years into her career, Kimmie welcomed into the world her first child, Luna. That was right around the time Kimmie and I first met. I had just begun my new consulting job, and the TV station where she worked became one of my primary clients.

I quickly recognized her as an overachiever and essential to the operation. In our first one-on-one meeting, I also sensed a certain level of stress that I have seen time and again among highly ambitious professionals; Kimmie was drowning in that familiar pool of too much to do and not enough time to do it in. She was working ten to twelve hours per day at the TV station, then going home to tackle her personal to-do list *and* find time to spend with her young daughter and husband.

At the time, her husband Mike openly questioned how long she would be able to continue at this pace. Her job, he thought, was "grinding her up." And it was a job that she loved.

"I would get so worked up because I wanted to do everything," Kimmie says now, looking back.[3] "I was tired and frustrated because I was working extra hours to get everything right, but that was just making me more tired and frustrated."

In most modern newsrooms, there are large-screen monitors displaying the analytics for how many people are viewing the news articles and videos in real-time. There are dashboards and regular reports sent to managers and the wider staff multiple times per day. As with so many modern companies, Kimmie explains, "Your identity is tied to the numbers and your self-worth is reflected in the reports." One of her professional priorities has always been to help people get the information they need. During public emergencies, content like Kimmie's can help save people's lives. When wildfires ravaged the Bay Area in 2018 and 2020, the analytics felt especially vital. Bigger numbers in those reports meant she was helping more people.

In early 2020, during the months of lockdown, Kimmie donned a mask and carted Luna around the Bay Area, delivering care packages to the members of the digital team she managed.

I helped the organization establish a new structure, and some new approaches that, in addition to some personnel changes, began to reframe what had been a difficult culture. Managing an organization's culture is a perpetual project, but this team was able to make significant progress at the outset.

When Kimmie and I met again, a year after our first conversation, she had every reason to be even more overwhelmed, not less. On top of the demands of a relentless daily news cycle, she had more work projects on her plate than ever. At home, she still had the responsibilities of parenting a two-year-old and keeping up with everything else. Despite this, Kimmie seemed happier and less stressed at work.

Kimmie had to learn new ways to balance work and home. Changes to the station's culture and organization, and improvement in what had been some tense relationship dynamics, had made a big difference in helping her find balance. As a result, she was able to find more meaning and joy in her job again.

"Things we wanted to change became possible," Kimmie says. "Putting people in the roles they were meant to be in [made] it easier on everyone. And motherhood puts things into perspective. Now my real job is raising this tiny human. Focusing on her helped me focus on myself."

Have you ever felt like you were "getting snappy" at work? That's how Kimmie describes the feeling of anxiety and being overwhelmed that manifests itself in being short with her colleagues. Most people mistakenly believe they can turn that off when they go home at the end of the day, but it's not that easy.

"If I'm not having a good day at work, it's coming out on [Luna]," says Kimmie, who added a sign near her computer to remind her: "This too shall pass." She says it has helped her maintain her perspective, and to trust that "everything's going to be OK."

The lessons in this book are meant to create more Kimmies. The way she described how her life had changed a year after we first met was one of the driving inspirations that led me to the concept of The Butterfly Impact. The seemingly small organizational and role changes at work created a ripple effect throughout the rest of Kimmie's life, positively impacting her family and others in her world.

What if you don't have control or influence on the culture where you work? Or a company transformation program to help you create the kind of systemic changes that helped Kimmie begin to thrive? You can still chart your own path, identifying and making small, positive adjustments at work which, in turn, will bring more happiness to the rest of your life. Remember, you can pull small levers to make positive changes in the world around you.

TIME FOR A RESET

In 2020, everything changed.

We can seize this rare, globally imposed reset to design our work world in a new way so that it gives us less stress, more validation, and more fulfillment. We can make a bigger impact as these personal changes reverberate through the lives of our co-workers, our leaders, our customers, and our families and communities.

When even one exchange between two people is more engaging and meaningful than those they've had in the past, those two people will move forward with feelings of greater purpose and validation, and less frustration and stress. When they in turn have a more engaging and meaningful exchange with two other co-workers, the benefits of this reset begin to spread through the organization. And when they take those feelings of increased validation and reduced stress into their lives outside of work and are better partners, parents, sons, daughters, and friends, the benefits spread even farther: they indirectly (and maybe unconsciously) contribute to building a better society, because they have more positives to contribute and fewer negatives to process. They have more time to see what's important, and more opportunities to give back to everyone who benefits from their unique talents and gifts.

This is The Butterfly Impact: our small personal changes lead to big impacts on those around us. More positive connections and fewer negative ones.

Changing corporate culture to improve everyone's overall well-being may feel like too big a lift. It's an overwhelming challenge to motivate people to make small changes in their lives for the greater good, especially if they don't feel any personal benefit. The secret of The Butterfly Impact is that it's all about personal motivations. The small changes you make will benefit you personally and improve your life immediately. This practical guide will help you be more productive and fulfilled at work, happier in life, more organized and less stressed overall.

"I think it's a greater sense of calm and ease" is how Kimmie characterizes her current work life.

Bob Chapman dreams of a world where we celebrate TGIM—

Thank Goodness It's Monday—instead of TGIF. "I get back to a place I feel valued, I get to contribute my gifts, I get to play the game of business with people," Chapman says. "The No. 1 source of happiness in the world is meaningful work in a company you feel respected in."

The butterfly is a symbol of resurrection. It represents endurance, change, hope, and life. We need all those things now, more than ever.

For many of us, work-life *balance* became work-life *blending* in 2020. The rest of this book will show you how to turn that into work-life *happiness*.

Let's make it happen.

PART 1

DO YOUR WORK DIFFERENTLY

CHAPTER 1

THE CULT OF BUSY

*Time is the singular measure of life. It's one of the few
things you cannot get more of. Knowing how to spend
it well is the most important skill you can have.*

—SCOTT BERKUN

Shauna Causey is an entrepreneur and the source of a torrent
of new ideas. Her charming smile, warm personality and infectious laugh are the first things that most people notice about her.
But they quickly learn that a creative brainstorm is constantly
churning in her mind, ready to explode with questions and
ideas for anyone who engages with her.

She is also ridiculously busy. In addition to working with startup
companies and constantly speaking at events, Shauna has served
on boards for community organizations and volunteered her time
in a variety of ways. She's constantly spitballing ideas with anyone
who will listen, looking for the next cool thing to throw her passion
into. In 2019 she was a partner at Madrona Venture Labs, a startup
incubator created by Seattle's top venture capital firm, doing what
good entrepreneurs do best: trying to solve her own problem.

A mom with two young kids, Shauna struggled to find childcare that offered the services and structured learning approaches she hoped for. She was frustrated from the outset of her childcare search: she kept landing on waitlists, and found few good options for solving one of the most important problems any new working parent faces.

She started building what she describes as an "Airbnb for childcare" to create private micro-schools in people's homes.[4] It would mean new opportunities for teachers and daycare professionals and, hopefully, help with her own childcare issues.

She launched Weekdays in March 2020, just as the pandemic and resulting lockdown shuttered many larger childcare facilities. Shauna's already over-subscribed life took a frenzied turn.

"I thought I knew what it was like to be a startup CEO," says Shauna, who has been involved with startup companies for more than a decade and counts many startup CEOs as friends.[5] "I discovered it's like going to Europe: people can try to explain it to you, but you don't really get it until you're actually there."

Her timing couldn't have been better—or worse. Interest in Weekdays from parents, teachers and daycare professionals surged. Meanwhile, Shauna had been trying to raise funding to get the company off the ground, but investors were suddenly preoccupied with trying to survive the pandemic. She was able to secure a loan through the Paycheck Protection Program (PPP) and put some of her own money into the company, but with only one web developer and barely any staff, the project quickly became overwhelming.

"We were getting thousands of phone calls," says Shauna, who set up a Google Voice account to manage the volume. Requests for media interviews were among the calls, so Shauna purchased a home light kit from Amazon and started waking up before dawn to speak to morning news shows across the nation on Zoom, including *The Today Show* and Bloomberg.

"Everyone suddenly wanted to know, 'what are micro-schools?'" says Shauna, who estimates she did around sixty interviews between TV, print, and radio outlets. She eventually hired a public relations firm to temporarily handle the requests. "It was a moment in time, and I tried to take advantage of that."

Meanwhile, she still had her own problem to solve: caring for four-year-old Connery and his one-year-old brother, Dylan, who had just started walking. She launched a Weekdays micro-school next door to her house, hired the teacher, and sent Connery to school with seven other kids while the pandemic continued to wreak havoc on school systems around the United States.

Shauna Causey and Connery

THE KEY TO ADDING VALUE TO THOSE AROUND YOU IS BEING INTENTIONAL ABOUT HOW YOU SPEND YOUR TIME, MAKING SURE THE MOST IMPORTANT ACTIVITIES ARE PRIORITIZED. KNOWING THIS IS ONE THING, BUT DOING IT REGULARLY IS SOMETHING ELSE ENTIRELY.

Balancing work and life is a big challenge for most people. In addition to those 90,000 hours spent "at the factory," the rest of our lives often demands that we juggle too many things at once. The interconnectedness of digital culture makes it easier than ever to spawn new ideas and, like Shauna, pursue them with passion. There's a downside, however, as people fill up their days and nights with activities and commitments, never-ending emails and Slack messages and social media rabbit holes without stopping to think about how they are spending their time.

"Before I had kids I could just work into the evening," Shauna says. "Now I just can't. I'm learning how to—well, I'm really being forced—to manage my time more effectively and simultaneously realizing how valuable my time is."

This is what author Scott Berkun calls "the cult of busy."

"The cult of busy explains the behavior of many people," Berkun wrote in *Mindfire: Big Ideas for Curious Minds*. "By appearing busy, others bother them less, and simultaneously believe they're doing well. It's quite a trick."

The key to adding value to those around you is being intentional about how you spend your time, making sure the most important activities are prioritized. Knowing this is one thing, but doing it regularly is something else entirely.

"Time is the singular measure of life," Berkun added. "It's one of the few things you cannot get more of. Knowing how to spend it well is the most important skill you can have."

I met Scott in 2009 at a Saturday conference he helped organize called Presentation Camp. I remember questioning whether spending a sunny spring day inside learning how to be a better presenter and speaker would be worthwhile. It was, if only for the opportunity to connect with Scott, and our paths have crossed several times since (he was even kind enough to help me navigate publishing the book you're now reading). I met Shauna in 2010 on a flight to Austin for SXSW Interactive conference; our seats were next to one another. "I think I follow you on Twitter," I said to her. "I think *I* follow *you* on Twitter," she replied. We've been friends ever since. Again, a worthwhile use of my time—networking on social media. But only to a point. I know I can't spend too much time going to weekend events and scrolling LinkedIn, Twitter, and Instagram. I can't afford it.

In 1748, Benjamin Franklin said, "Time is money," and that phrase has been repeated countless times since.[6] If that saying is true, then consider the concept of "time affluence." If we treat our time like we treat our money, as something to save, invest and spend on the most important things in life, we can be more disciplined, organized and productive. We can also be happier. Even happier than if we had more money.

"In general, those who are valuing time are overall happier than those who value money," says Yale professor Laurie Santos, host of *The Happiness Lab* podcast. "What we're finding is prioritizing getting extra time and doing less stuff, but having more time, is better than the happiness associated with money."[7]

The word "affluence" comes from the Latin verb *affluere*, which means "to flow abundantly." How much time each day would it take for you to feel "time affluent"? The pandemic hit the pause button on the cult of busy—a longer pause than most of us wanted, but one of the silver linings from 2020 is the extra time that we were given. The quarantines and canceled events, the absence of work travel, kids' sports, vacations, and so much more in 2020 gave many people a chance to feel time affluent, maybe for the first time.

"One of my favorite sayings is that being here is enough," Deepak Chopra wrote in *The Ultimate Happiness Prescription*.[8] "When people hear this, particularly successful people whose lives are full of projects and accomplishments, they look confused.

"As they pursue lives that are so full of activity and goals, most people are not fulfilling their being. Quite the opposite. They are running away from a deep-seated fear that life is empty unless you constantly fill it up."

The cult of busy taxes your emotional well-being. Time is finite, and the more you try to jam into an hour, an afternoon, or a day, the less affluent you feel, and the more your brain processes disappointment with all that you are *not* doing. Your mental to-do list is nothing more than a series of agreements you are making—and too often breaking—with yourself, which is not a great foundation for a healthy relationship.

BUTTERFLY IMPACT SIGNPOST

Time. Stress. Productivity. Relationships. All of this and more has helped build the multi-billion-dollar self-help industry, which is now powered by infomercials, smartphone apps, personal coaching, motivational speakers and, of course, books.

Yet self-help is selfish. That's how it feels for many of us, given how low on the priority list it often falls because, well, we're just too busy. After the workday is done, the domestic demands begin. How do you find time to invest in yourself?

Here's the secret: making positive changes in how you spend your workday is a force multiplier. It will influence and impact your relationships and your productivity at work and have a ripple effect through your relationships and productivity away from the job. It's more effective to find workplace happiness and carry it through your personal life than the other way around. These are some of the small levers you can pull to engage The Butterfly Impact in your life.

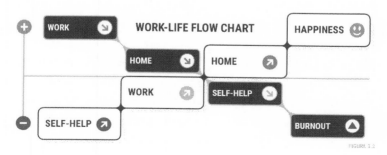

FIGURE 3.2

"I didn't want to live a life where my happiness is completely dependent on work," says Shauna, who started noticing people in her life that fell into that trap. "For some people, if work isn't going well then everything else was in the drain.

"[Seeing that] helped me reveal how much value I'm getting out of different things in my life. I came to realize what those things are—what is going to be meaningful."

I first learned about this lesson in a windowless conference room, nearly twenty years ago. It was one of those all-day trainings with the uncomfortable chairs, stale coffee, and random candy in little bowls on the tables to help you get through hours of PowerPoint slides. Most of the material in these sessions was quickly forgotten, but I remember this one. At least one key point, anyway, and I often use it to this day.

It was from a program based on the popular Stephen Covey book *7 Habits of Highly Effective People*, and I think of it as big rocks and a jar.

The conference presenter played a video showing someone dumping a mix of big and small rocks out of a jar and then attempting to put them all back in.[9] The unsuspecting victim of this demonstration scoops the pebbles together with her hands and then pours them into the jar. Then tries to jam the big rocks down between them. It doesn't work.

The jar is a metaphor for life. It's the big rocks in your life that should be the priority. All the little rocks have to fall around them to fit into the jar. You need to address the big rocks—the most important three to five things in your life—first. The rest is just gravel. If you try to fill the jar with the little rocks, sand and pebbles first, the big rocks won't fit.

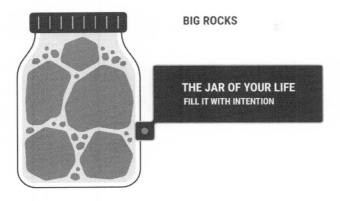

BIG ROCKS

THE JAR OF YOUR LIFE
FILL IT WITH INTENTION

FIGURE 3.3

Do you ever feel like you're spending too much time on the little rocks? Or not enough on the big rocks?

Focusing on the big rocks is what Greg McKeown calls *essentialism* (he published a book in 2018 with that title). It's not about how to get more things done; it's about how to get the right things done. "It doesn't mean just doing less for the sake of less either," McKeown wrote. "It is about making the wisest possible investment of your time and energy in order to operate at our highest point of contribution by doing only what is essential."

Thinking of time as an investment makes sense. Evaluating the return on investment (ROI) of your time will help you view your mornings, your evenings, and your weekends differently. What are your big rocks? How much return do you get from spending time on them compared to the gravel? The pebbles? The sand?

In other words, what would you rather be: crazy busy or time affluent?

Since becoming a parent and a startup CEO, Shauna has learned to experiment with different ways to manage her time. She measures the ROI, budgeting her time the same way a company would budget its expenses and other resources. While she considered herself busy before, the pandemic world of 2020 taught her how to value her time differently.

"I would work all day, then eat dinner, then continue working. I didn't have a lot of balance," she says, adding that the way she uses her time now is "absolutely more meaningful."

One more thing: "You gotta take care of yourself," Shauna says. "You have to realize you have limits."

This is the essence of The Butterfly Impact: understanding your limits with work and life, making the most of your time and prioritizing your work-life happiness first. Knowing *why* you need to think differently about work-life happiness will help you understand *how* to act differently. With more focus. More intention. And more ease.

That will lead to more meaning and fulfillment in your work and your life.

CHAPTER 2

WHAT DOES HAPPINESS HAVE TO DO WITH WORK?

Happiness is a skill, not just a feeling, and you can strengthen that skill with practice.

—NATALY KOGAN

Kellie Garnett has always been tense. When she was in the first grade, she rarely smiled. She remained focused on doing well in class, following the rules, pleasing the teacher, and getting good grades. She couldn't relax, even though her parents tried to help her calm down and find some joy. They created a chart and would add a gold star to it every time she smiled. Ten stars meant a Disney movie in a big theater with popcorn. This little game of motivation gave her incentive to smile. It also taught her an important lesson: positivity takes persistence. After all, happiness is an accomplishment.

Flash forward, many years later, and Kellie is all grown up and running the editorial meeting each morning at KING 5, the NBC affiliate TV station in Seattle. She's doing it with a smile and laughter—and Fun Fact Friday. Each week she invests a few minutes to research and deliver a fun fact to the daily gathering of skeptical, curmudgeonly journalists, TV producers, and managers. Often these facts are related to one of the people in the meeting and usually a fun surprise for everyone else. By doing this, she literally forces happiness into the workday, if only once a week.

As someone who attended these meetings, I always appreciated her effort.

Her transformation didn't happen by accident. She remade her approach to life and work with intention and effort.

"I was tired of listening to my negative thoughts, tired of the self-imposed pressure," Kellie told me.[10] "I wanted a better outlook and a more enjoyable life. So, I made a conscious decision to try to be more positive. Knowing myself, I figured it would be impossible to change. But I was determined to see if I could fake it until I made it. And that's just what happened."

Kellie Garnett

Kellie's transformation didn't happen overnight. By the time she was doing Fun Fact Friday, she was fifteen years into her career at the local TV newsroom. She had started as an intern; when I met her, she was managing a team of investigative reporters. They were experienced, well-respected journalists who had a strong sense of purpose. They pursued tips that would often lead to stories revealing fraud, government waste, even corruption. When the daily news required coverage of some of the community's highest-profile events, the investigative reporters joined in to help. Often, those events were gloomy. When Kellie was promoted to manager, it was an environment desperate for positivity.

She started small, giving an encouraging word to a videographer whose computer crashed on an edit in the final moments before the 5 p.m. newscast, or flashing a quick smile at the assignment editor drowning in police-scanner noise, with two phones to her ears. When she saw that her boss was under the pressure, Kellie gave him a pat on the back to show him that she believed in him.

"I'm not exaggerating when I say I could actually see the softening of their faces when that positive energy hit their hearts. And I felt better, too," Kellie says.

She tested it out in meetings, mentally adding time to the agenda for a joke or story about the latest trial or tribulation that still worked out in the end. When she took over the morning editorial meetings for the newsroom, she tried to infuse her passion for the work as the team ground through assignments and decisions. She recognized a great headline written by a digital producer, or a creative stand-up by a reporter. She started Fun Fact Friday as a chance to surprise even the savviest of journalists with a gem of knowledge.

"No matter how tense it got, or how much pressure I felt, I tried to stay positive," she says. "When a story would fall through or there was a big mistake on the air, I sensed my colleagues looking at me, deciding how they should feel about it. Just like when my daughter plays basketball, trips and falls, screeching across the court. That moment of silence when she searches the bleachers for my face and we lock eyes. I mouth to her, 'You're alright. You got this. Shake it off.' Inside I'm dying, but outside, I'm positive. You're okay. We're okay."

Powered by this newfound positivity, Kellie's professional growth exploded. In 2016, Kellie made a huge career change and joined Starbucks as editor-in-chief of the company's blog, *1912 Pike*. A couple years later, she jumped to a better opportunity at Amazon, and in 2020 was promoted to the title of Principal of Strategic Communication for Alexa Everywhere.

"It's important to know that my words were authentic and from the heart. What was not natural was finding the positive first," she told me. "Worry and fear were inherently my motivators. I started with the positive. And life got better. I liked being positive. I saw the impact on others, then I saw the transformation in me. The cloud of distress lifted, and work was much more fun. And I believe I was more effective. No longer weighed down by dread, I thought bigger, and encouraged others to think bigger, too. Anything became possible. Instead of reasons to say no, I was finding it easier to say, let's try it."

Being positive at work can have a ripple effect through a team and organization. It can also lead to increased happiness outside of work, and serve as a force of change in people's lives in a way that few other emotions can do.

While it often gets overlooked, positivity not only belongs in the workplace—it deserves priority. We all learn about the American right to "life, liberty and the pursuit of happiness" in grade school. But Thomas Jefferson's 1776 phrase never seemed to apply to work. Throughout the Colonial Era, the Industrial Revolution, and today's age of Wall Street profit-seeking and digital productivity, the connection between happiness and work has remained elusive. We often think of them as mutually exclusive: At work? Not happy. Away from work? Happy.

The target of Jefferson's *pursuit* has often been construed to mean *property, wealth* or *success*, which all too often have been understood as the drivers of happiness. Multiple studies have found, however, that the opposite is true.

 **BUTTERFLY IMPACT SIGNPOST**

As Kellie's experience illustrates, true happiness at work is not only possible—it will improve your overall health and well-being. The first step to making that happen is to simply open your mind to the possibility that it *could* happen. The next step is to make it happen.

Too often, we let work happen to us. Our calendars tell us what meetings to attend. Our emails tell us what questions to answer. Our team leaders tell us what the priority is today. If we let work happen to us, we often feel helpless and unfulfilled.

It's all about our mindset. Stanford professor Carol Dweck's research has taught millions the power of developing a "growth mindset" instead of accepting a "fixed mindset."[11] One of the most powerful parts of this concept is also incredibly simple: you can change your mindset, just like Kellie did over the years in her various roles and jobs.

"Just by knowing about the two mindsets, you can start thinking and reacting in new ways," Dweck writes. "People tell me that they start to catch themselves when they are in the throes of the fixed mindset—passing up a chance for learning, feeling labeled by a failure, or getting discouraged when something requires a lot of effort. And then they switch themselves into the growth mindset—making sure they take the challenge, learn from the failure, or continue their effort."

With the power to change your mindset, you can tap into what author Shawn Achor calls "The Happiness Advantage," a conclusion he's drawn from more than 200 scientific studies on nearly 275,000 people.[12]

"Based on the wealth of data [the researchers] compiled, they found that happiness *causes* success and achievement, not the other way around," Achor writes in his 2010 book *The Happiness Advantage*. "Happy workers have higher levels of productivity, produce higher sales, perform better in leadership positions, and receive higher performance ratings and higher pay."

While this sounds too good to be true, it's real. Kellie's career path is proof. Veering from journalism and the one place she had worked in her career provided an opportunity to use her powers of positivity.

"It was universally accepted, a language and attitude that opened doors with almost everyone I met," Kellie says. "And those that were resistant often came around, when they trusted my words weren't hollow platitudes but real talk."

The obvious question is, then: how do we make ourselves happy, especially in a world as unsettled and ominous as the one we are living in now?

The short answer is that we have to prioritize it and work at it. It all comes down to habits, those little things we do regularly that make us who we are. As I tell my teenage sons, it's not what you *say* or what you *know*, it's what you *do* that makes you who you are. *I'm not saying they listen to me, but that's what I tell them.*

"Happiness is a skill, not just a feeling, and you can strengthen that skill with practice," says Nataly Kogan, author of *Happier Now*.[13] Kogan immigrated to the United States as a refugee from the former Soviet Union when she was thirteen years old and started her new life in the projects outside of Detroit. She battled her way up the corporate ladder and became a venture capitalist at the age of twenty-six before building Happier.com, her consultancy, which helps companies with emotional health skills at work.

Think about that for a moment: Kogan built a highly successful business career after starting out in a life of poverty. She could have pursued pretty much anything, and she decided to help people understand the power and importance of happiness. I think it's awesome, and, like Kellie's story, an inspiration to make happiness a priority in your own life.

MAKING IT HAPPEN

What is happiness? Most people don't spend much time thinking about it. You just know it when you feel it. It is often associated with something happening to you, like receiving a gift, winning a game or getting a new pair of shoes. In the context of work, though, it should be seen as a direction instead of destination.

According to Barbara Fredrickson, there are ten feelings associated with happiness. Fredrickson is a psychology professor at the University of North Carolina and author of several books, including *Positivity: Top-Notch Research That Reveals the 3-to-1 Ratio That Will Change Your Life*.[14]

Start by focusing on these ten feelings during your workday. To establish a habit of happiness, select one attribute for each day of the week. If that's too ambitious to start, pick one per week.

For example:

- **Joy.** A great cup of coffee, a favorite food for lunch, the right song in your headphones—you can find joy through simple moments, if you start looking for them.

- **Gratitude.** Thank someone for a job well done, or for just being themselves and showing up.

- **Serenity.** Find ten minutes for peace and quiet and reflection. Listen to a meditation exercise on your phone, if that's something you enjoy.

- **Interest.** Learn something new about a teammate or a project or product at work.

- **Hope.** Peek ahead on your work calendar to find an event or a meeting that you are looking forward to. Or a project or a milestone that is near completion.

- **Pride.** Share a cool project or outcome with a friend or colleague, or post it to LinkedIn.

- **Amusement.** Introduce something fun into your work conversation. Start a meeting with a funny story or image or meme. Post a joke to your favorite Slack channel.

- **Inspiration.** Find a work-related article on Medium or LinkedIn that inspires you and share it with your colleagues.

- **Awe.** Take a nature break or walk outside, and look closely at the trees and birds.

- **Love.** You might not think that love has a place at work, but start paying attention to how often this word is used during the workday. Start saying it yourself. "I love that!" is a great piece of feedback on a colleague's project.

This is how Fun Fact Friday came about for Kellie. While she didn't carry that practice forward to her new roles at Starbucks and Amazon, she adopted new habits for happiness. When I worked with Kellie, we were managing a digital news team at a local TV station in Seattle. Everyone was frequently overworked, underappreciated, and stressed by working on a seemingly constant flow of negative news. Kellie always remained positive and brought an uplifting energy to the team and the rest of the newsroom. As she explained, it didn't come naturally. She worked hard to cultivate her positive powers.

"Being positive and encouraging others is now my favorite thing to do. It's who I am," she says. "I still deal with my natural inclination of worry and anxiety. But sooner than later, the fog is lifted. When the world is dark, being a voice of hope is like water in a desert. I'm so thankful I get to try and quench their thirst. Gold stars for everyone!"

Happiness makes you a better performer at work and more successful in your life. While you can't push an easy button and make a great day happen at work each day, you can start building small habits that infuse moments of happiness into your workday, increasing the chances of having more great days and fewer bad ones.

CHAPTER 3

CHANGE THE WAY YOU CHANGE

If information was the answer, then we'd
all be billionaires with perfect abs.

—DEREK SIVERS

Mark Mohammadpour calls it one of the worst experiences of his life. In 2006, as an award-winning public relations executive, he embarked on a press tour that would take him to three cities in five days. On a cross-country flight from Portland, Oregon, to New York City, he was stuck in a middle seat, weighing 350 pounds, and he felt miserable, unhealthy, and concerned for his physical well-being.

"I couldn't even walk up a flight of stairs," Mark told me.[15] "Colleagues were calling me Eeyore because I was so depressed."

Mark knew he needed to change. After trying every method available, he says that small, incremental, and sustainable changes over time led to his mental and physical transformation. He shed 110 pounds over nine months and went from a size fifty waist to a thirty-four. He has kept the weight off, losing a total of 150 pounds over the years.

His own success and passion for fitness inspired him to become a certified personal trainer and health coach. Knowing firsthand the challenges that PR workers face, he knew they needed help. (A 2019 CareerCast survey ranked public relations executive among the top ten most stressful jobs along with airline pilot, police officer, and firefighter.) He saw an opportunity to help people he knew well, whom he had been working with for years, who were struggling with work, life, and health. He launched Chasing the Sun, his consultancy to help individuals and organizations transform.

"You have to build confidence and resilience, and be mentally and physically strong," says Mark, who did twenty-five health and wellness workshops for organizations in 2020. It has been a natural progression for Mark, who took pride in the way he managed and led his team all those years as a PR executive. "As much as I was an advocate of the clients, I was focused on the development of the professionals, and I was there to help guide them, set them up for success, and then get out of the way."

The biggest change, according to Mark, is what he has learned: that prioritizing his own health and wellness has allowed him to support those around him at an even higher level. This is The Butterfly Impact in action.

Mark Mohammadpour posing in his old jeans.

"I found my purpose," Mark says. "I realized this is my life. I told myself: You better figure out a way to enjoy that time. I care about the work experiences, I care about the relationships, and am now ultimately happier because of how I'm helping others."

Change is always a challenge. In work and life, many changes are extrinsic and out of your control. When your boss changes the weekly staff meeting to 8 a.m. on Mondays, you are forced to adapt. You have no choice. Other changes, like the ones Mark made in his life, are intrinsic and come from your own needs or wants for your life. If you are pursuing true work-life happiness, you'll need to be good at both work and life.

In 2006 I was working on my first book, hoping to teach journalists working for legacy newspaper, TV, and radio operations to open their minds and embrace the digital disruption that was starting to wash over them. At the time, Twitter didn't exist, and the iPhone hadn't been invented yet. The internet had already changed so much of daily life: dealing with constant emails, uploading photos to Flickr, watching videos on YouTube, and answering questions with Google and Wikipedia. It seemed obvious that more changes—and bigger changes—were on the way.

I have spent the last twenty years trying to help people do their jobs differently. It's never easy. While some people are naturally curious and interested in the next new thing, others prefer consistency, and would rather things just stay the same as they are today. I wanted to understand what leads those people to resist change so I could find a way to help them become more open to it.

I learned about *temporary incompetence*, which is one of the main reasons people resist change, especially at work. No one wants to feel incompetent, especially in jobs where ego plays a part. When there's a new way of doing something, it's natural that people will have to learn something new. For example, if the company you work for introduces a new way to request vacation time, you will have to learn something new if you want to make that annual summer trek to the beach. The first time you try to navigate the new computer interface, you will feel a bit lost, confused, and maybe even frustrated. That feeling of incompetence is what drives people to resist change, even though the distress is temporary.

The problem, of course, is that change is *inevitable*. It's coming no matter how much you resist it. Getting comfortable with change means being willing to be uncomfortable. The discomfort is temporary, and the benefits are often long lasting (as in greater productivity, connectedness, education, etc.). Change requires us to step out of our comfort zone. That alone is beneficial.

BUTTERFLY IMPACT SIGNPOST

The Butterfly Impact of successfully navigating and creating positive changes at work is priceless. In working with dozens of organizations over the past few years, I have seen stark differences between those that embrace and celebrate change and those that struggle with it. Multiple studies have found that the organizations that embrace change and adapt relatively easily are routinely ranked high in "best places to work" surveys, at the same time performing at higher levels than their competition.

To fully thrive, you need to accept two facts:

1. **Change is inevitable.** Things around you—at work and at home—are always changing, and how you deal with and accept those changes matters a lot.

2. **Progress is optional.** How *you* create change, the kind of change that leads to growth, matters even more.

There is a fundamental dynamic at work that impacts both aspects of change. Think of it as a tug-of-war between two parts of your brain: the rational (thinking) side and the emotional (feeling) side. The better you understand how this dynamic works for you, the better at change you will be.

In other words, it's like riding an elephant.

Psychologist Jonathan Haidt first used this metaphor in his book, *The Happiness Hypothesis*. Chip and Dan Heath expanded on it in *Switch: How to Change When Change is Hard*, one of the best books on change you can read.[16] "Change isn't an event, it's a process," the Heath brothers write. "When people try to change things, they're usually tinkering with behaviors that have become automatic, and changing those behaviors requires careful supervision."

They explain how the Rider, who has many strengths, represents the rational part of your brain. Most importantly, the Rider is a thinker and planner who can plot a better future. The Elephant represents the emotional side, and tends to go wherever the hell it wants—sometimes, that's nowhere at all. To make positive changes, the Rider must guide the Elephant. The metaphor works because we all know how powerful our emotions can be. *Deciding to drink a green smoothie in the morning is the rational choice, but eating that glazed donut sounds way better.*

Try to see the change coming at you, or the change you are trying to create, through this lens. In teaching journalists over the years to incorporate social media into their workflow, for example, I emphasized the potential for their work to reach more people if they post links on Facebook or Twitter. I know that most journalists are motivated by uncovering important information and telling compelling stories, so the explanation that these new platforms could bring more audience to their work helps satisfy both the Rider and the Elephant. It makes sense and feels gratifying.

It also helps to highlight "bright spots," those examples of things that are going well, or at least in the direction you want. When you celebrate the bright spots, even when they are few and far between, you make it easier for your Rider to think through shaping the Path. And you make the emotional side of your brain, your Elephant, more excited about the change at hand.

Bright spots also illustrate how the perception of change is essential. Luc de Brabendere, author of *The Forgotten Half of Change*, offers a complementary framework.[17] "If you want to change, you have to change twice," he says. The first change is simply imagination. You invent the future state in your mind. The second is actually carrying out the change you envisioned.

This is how I approached my teenage sons when discussing their lackluster academic performance over the years. "I'm not a good student" was the message I was hearing whenever the issue of grades came up. And while we discussed the practical changes that could be made—structured study time, tutoring, working with teachers after class—I tried to explain that none of it would truly make a difference until they could see themselves as "good students." It's the perception that is "the forgotten half," so I asked them to pretend they got an A or B in a certain class and actually imagine how it would feel to score those marks.

This technique of changing your perception can work in all facets of life, whether you're learning a new software program at work, trying to lose weight, or starting a meditation practice. You must *see* the change before you can *be* the change. This will help make the concrete steps needed to perform the change *feel* more attainable, which helps the Rider guide the Elephant.

This is especially effective at work, where people want to be seen as talented, valuable, and, at minimum, competent in their jobs. Asking them to learn a new skill or software program may trigger their feelings of temporary incompetence—and plunge them into the "Valley of Despair."

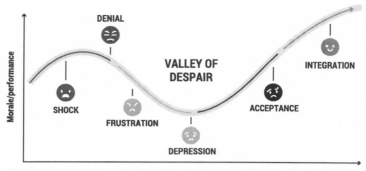

Have you ever been in the Valley? I hope so, because it's where growth happens. But it's also where people often give up, frustrated with the feeling of incompetence and the feeling that "this will never work" or "I will never learn this." The key is to make this incompetence *temporary*; you have to keep pushing through the Valley to get to the other side.

"Oh man, I'm in the Valley right now!" one manager quipped upon learning about the Valley in one of my workshops on leading change. "Me, too!" replied one of the others in a roomful of managers. Every time I introduce the Valley of Despair to a group, at least a few people light up with recognition and relief. There's something cathartic about knowing that feeling incompetent is a shared experience and totally normal. Then we talk through how to help each other push through the Valley to the other side. It takes systematic training, planning, support, and encouragement.

Creating such a system works well when you have a team of caring managers and a management consultant to help you through the Valley—not to mention the motivation of continued employment. But how do you apply this to your attempts at personal change, when it's just you, in the Valley, alone?

The best approach is to make the change as small as possible.

The Heath brothers call it "shrinking the change." An abundance of research will show you the power of creating small changes and turning them into habits and routines. There is also abundant wisdom from the authors of books on this topic, including:

- "First, never underestimate the power of inertia. Second, that power can be harnessed," write Cass Sunstein and Richard Thaler in *Nudge: Improving Decisions About Health, Wealth and Happiness.* (Their insights about the value of a "nudge" to bring about change won them the Nobel prize in economics.)

- "Behavior change is a skill...but as you practice it, it becomes second nature—just like driving," says B. J. Fogg in *Tiny Habits: The Small Changes That Change Everything.*

- "Some people spend their entire lives waiting for the time to be right to make an improvement," observes James Clear in *Atomic Habits: An Easy & Proven Way to Build Good Habits & Break Bad Ones.*

- "If you believe you can change—if you make it a habit—the change becomes real," writes Charles Duhigg in *The Power of Habit.*

The common thread that runs through all this is that to do *something*, however small, is the best way to start to change. Then develop a system you can repeat consistently. This is also the foundation for The Butterfly Impact: small, specific changes, aimed to create a ripple effect downstream that becomes increasingly significant.

I finally found my way to fitness more than twenty years ago via a goal of going to the gym once a week. I had previously tried a few New Year's resolutions, and audacious new fitness plans that began with five days a week of working out. All of them failed. Benjamin Hardy knows why.

"Your willpower is gone. It was gone the moment you woke up and got sucked back into your smartphone," Hardy wrote in *Willpower Doesn't Work*.[18] "White-knuckling your way to change doesn't work. It never did. Instead, you need to create and control your environment."

One day a week was easy and attainable. Within a month I was going a second day each week. Then three times, then four. Today I'm active or exercising five to six days a week, and have been for more than a decade. It all started with that one day a week. Just like Mark Mohammadpour, I found that small, incremental, and sustainable changes made a huge impact.

When you think about it, change is just a mind game. You could even shrink the change further and start your workout plan with a goal of simply putting your workout clothes on in the morning. Just that small change—getting out of your comfies and into your jogging shoes—will make it easier to actually go to the gym or outside for a walk or jog. Each time you do, celebrate this "bright spot," so your Rider can continue guiding your Elephant in the right direction.

MAKING IT HAPPEN

Are you someone who likes change, or tries to avoid it? No matter where you land on the spectrum of embracing change, you can learn to make it work more effectively in your life, whether at work or outside of work. Here's how to get started:

- **Imagine.** How will the change feel once you make it? (Channel your inner athlete here: visualizing success has proven to be an effective tool in sports psychology.)

- **Shrink the Change.** What is the smallest thing you can *do regularly* to get started?

- **Set yourself up for success.** What can you change in your environment to help the change?

- **Find bright spots.** Celebrate your wins, and socialize them if possible.

You can read all the research you want, but in the end, it's the *doing* that matters. As Derek Sivers once said, "If more information was the answer, then we'd all be billionaires with perfect abs."[19]

CHAPTER 4

YOUR VALUES DRIVE HAPPINESS

*The fact that you're unhappy at work is a sign
that something is wrong. And if there's not a
values alignment, that's the breaking point.*

—LIZ PEARCE

Early in his career, Paolo Mottola worked for a large advertising and marketing agency in Seattle, and thought he had it made. The work seemed interesting enough and, combined with the flashy offices, free coffee (which was actually good), and downtown location next to cool bars and restaurants, what wasn't to like?

Oh, and the best perk of all? Happy hours!

"It seemed very cool to me as a young person who'd only recently gotten legal access to bars," Paolo says.[20] "You feel like, 'Wow, I'm really blending work and play.'"

As time went on, however, Paolo felt a disconnect. All the classic agency perks, which were similar to those his friends around town enjoyed at big tech companies and fast-moving startups, felt good in the moment, because everyone else seemed happy to have them. Yet, he thought, there must be more to work and life than this. Eventually Paolo landed a job at REI. The outdoor gear and clothing cooperative was founded by twenty-three climbing friends in the shadow of Mount Rainier in 1938. Its mission is to help people choose life outdoors.

He connected to the mission—and values—of REI. Much more than he did to happy hours and free snacks.

"I didn't realize how satisfying it would be to intermingle the feel-good benefits of a mission-based organization with work like this," says Paolo, who eventually helped develop and launch one of the best values-based marketing campaigns ever.

In 2015, as the Christmas shopping season approached, the company faced a challenge: "How does REI compete around a holiday that has created over-consumerism inconsistent with our core values?" Paolo says, "The answer: We don't."

As a retail store, REI could have followed conventional business logic suggesting that it extend in-store hours, mark down merchandise, and spend more on marketing and advertising than at any other time of the year. That's what the retail giants did every year. Instead, REI chose a different path.

"We decided to close on Black Friday to act on our values and, at the very least, give our store employees the day off. Many of them are career retail employees who hadn't had Thanksgiving and Black Friday off in years," Paolo told me. (REI has more than

12,000 employees.) "We're a brand that tells people to go outside to find their best selves, not wait outside for a doorbuster."

Paolo's team created the #OptOutside hashtag on social media to invite America to join them. More a movement than a campaign, it generated national media attention and social media buzz worth millions of dollars more than what it could have spent on its own.

It wasn't about the free marketing, however. It wasn't really even about Black Friday. The company made a decision to live its values in a very big and very intentional way. Imagine how employees felt, the day they learned they would be getting paid to go play outside.

Paolo Mottola

"It's a way different perk than a margarita cart," says Paolo, who is now the director of content and media at REI. "People feel they can bring more of themselves into the work. Outdoors as a lifestyle is something we embrace. It encourages people to be their fullest selves."

A small but humorous example of the REI culture is Paolo's voicemail recording on his phone, which simply says: "Hey Scott, leave a message." Since he works with a team of millennials who only text and don't leave voicemails, Paolo says he personalized his recording for the one friend who actually leaves a voicemail. "That's who I am."

 **BUTTERFLY IMPACT SIGNPOST**

People who are happy and satisfied at work are more likely to feel that their personal values match the values of the organization that employs them. Seems pretty obvious, right? Unfortunately, most people do not fall into this group. Why is that?

First and foremost, they have to know what their personal core values actually are. Most people can probably generalize, or make educated guesses as to their values, but the real answer to the question "What are my personal values?" takes work.

Next, while mission statements and key performance indicators are prevalent in most organizations today, core values that guide day-to-day decisions and activities can be a little more elusive. The corporate values movement largely began in 1994, thanks to the book *Built to Last*, leading companies to develop them, frame them, and hang them on the walls of the corporate offices. Those same companies have often had trouble actually living by them, however.

"The values fad swept through corporate America like chicken pox through a kindergarten class," Patrick Lencioni wrote for the *Harvard Business Review*, adding that 80 percent of the *Fortune* 100 tout their values publicly—values that too often stand for nothing but "a desire to be au courant or, worse still, politically correct."[21]

Often, it's because the core values that were chosen sound good in theory but don't help people make decisions and take actions each day. And that's the whole point of core values. Or, worse, the values that are framed on the wall say one thing and the people making decisions for the organization do something else.

"If you're not willing to accept the pain real values incur, don't bother going to the trouble of formulating a values statement," Lencioni wrote. "You'll be better off without one."

For example, you would expect a big pharmacy chain to focus on "helping people on their path to better health." That is the mission statement that CVS hung on its wall and published on its website. Yet, until a few years ago, the company sold cigarettes and tobacco products in its stores, as did other big pharmacy chains like Walgreens and Rite Aid (which have similar mission statements). Then, in 2014, CVS made the decision to live up to its values statement and stopped selling cigarettes and tobacco products.[22] (Neither of its major competitors, Rite Aid and Walgreens, followed suit.) The effect on sales revenue was a loss of around $2 billion each year. But the right thing to do for the organization was to live the values it espoused.

Values aren't values until they cost money or cause pain. As an individual, the cost of following your values is the financial risk of leaving one job for another, as Paolo did, or starting your own company, as Nicole Thomas did.

Nicole, whose story we will visit again in Chapter 16, switched industries, and found a position as vice president that gave her the opportunity to learn, grow, and lead a team spanning five states. She excelled, and soon came up for a promotion to become a senior vice president. Instead, she resigned and launched her own agency. Nicole was also teaching at a university and accepting speaking engagements around the country. In 2020, as the Black Lives Matter movement compelled companies to reconcile their espoused values with their practices, she found new opportunities to leverage her marketing and communication skills to help organizations craft authentic messages of diversity and inclusion they could live up to.

"The company's values didn't align with my values," Nicole told me about one of her previous jobs. "I had a great team, and it was doing pretty well, but you can't expect me to say things that are not true."

A classic example of this disconnect is Enron, which famously bilked investors out of millions of dollars before imploding in one of the biggest corporate scandals in US history. The company's values? Communication. Respect. Excellence. And— wait for it—*Integrity*, which the company described in its 2000 annual report as, "We work with customers and prospects openly, honestly, and sincerely." *Wow*.

KILLER VALUES

When Amy Balliett realized the infographic company she founded didn't align with her own values, it came with a "powder-keg moment." The short story is that an email that she intended to go only to her executive team went to all staff instead. It was "an angry email," according to Amy, and drove her and her entire team to have a "come-to-Jesus moment."

"We needed to develop our secret sauce—to identify the values of the company in a way that every person can recite. And then hire and fire employees and clients based on those values," Amy told me.[23] "Our values were defined, but not a single person could recite them."

Given the company's name at the time—Killer Infographics—and since it was a creative company, Amy and her team built out an acronym for "KILLER" to anchor the company's values in the company's name. They are:

- Keep learning

- Inspire others

- Lead by example

- Love what we do

- Embrace change

- Respect others

"Unless you're actively living those values, they don't matter," Amy told me, adding that the company identified the people who didn't live up to these values and gave them exit plans—including her business partner. The company has also developed a system to identify employees who have lived a core value, and the person with the most nominations each month receives recognition and a gift. It's important to celebrate the people and their actions that align with your organization's values, too.

Amy Balliett

Killer was employing around thirty people and bringing in almost $3 million in 2019 when—on Amy's thirty-seventh birthday—she sold the company to Los Angeles-based LRW Group. The company changed its name to Killer Visual Strategies to more fully encompass its services and capabilities and remains independently operated, with Amy still at the helm. This allows her to continue to enforce the values the company had established after that powder-keg moment.

It starts with how the company hires new employees, a process that is affectionately known as "the gauntlet." It takes six weeks to three months and includes multiple phone interviews and homework assignments—including questions on the Killer values. Before a prospective hire comes in for the first in-person interview, Amy and her team have already assessed the candidate's values for fit. This is followed by four hours of skills assessment, discussion of conflict resolution, and one-on-one "shoot the shit" time with Amy.

"I want to make sure this person feels comfortable speaking their mind," Amy told me. "We are very vulnerable and very transparent with each other. Everybody really aligns. It doesn't matter what your political beliefs or job roles [are]…That level of respect really resonates."

The first step is identifying your own personal core values. You need to know what you're trying to align. Once you have identified your values, match them up with what your organization lists as its values. Find the common ground, and make sure you understand which direction on your compass you are driving toward.

Your best opportunity for work-life happiness comes from a job that consistently allows you to use your unique talents and qualities to help a team and an organization move forward—in a direction that aligns with your core values.

YOUR BEST OPPORTUNITY FOR WORK-LIFE HAPPINESS COMES FROM A JOB THAT CONSISTENTLY ALLOWS YOU TO USE YOUR UNIQUE TALENTS AND QUALITIES TO HELP A TEAM AND AN ORGANIZATION MOVE FORWARD——IN A DIRECTION THAT ALIGNS WITH YOUR CORE VALUES.

If you are now thinking, *That's great, but what if I work for a company that doesn't align with my values?* Or, *doesn't live the values it hangs on the wall or publishes on the website?* The first step is identifying your own personal core values. You need to know what you're trying to align to.

Once you have identified your own core values, match them up with what your organization lists as its values. Find the common ground and make that your compass to chart the direction you are driving toward. Your best opportunity for work-life happiness comes from a job that consistently allows you to use your unique talents and qualities to help a team and an organization move forward—in a direction that aligns with your core values.

MAKING IT HAPPEN

Whether you work for an organization that has values that it lives by or not, you can improve your sense of validation and value by identifying your own core values. If you can match some to your organization, even better.

Here's a simple (but not always easy) way to do this:

- Do an online search for a list of personal core values (there are more than 200 on some lists).

- Pick from the list of core values and select your top ten.

- Look at those ten and take away five.

- Look at those five and take away two. Remember, these do not represent everything you value. These are your CORE values. Three is all you get.

A warning: this is not easy. My attempt at this while writing this chapter produced seventeen values for my first list. Seventeen! Eventually I pared it down to ten, then five, then three. Here is what that process looked like:

First pass: adaptability, balance, community, compassion, curiosity, diversity, enthusiasm, family, freedom, gratitude, generosity, happiness, health, integrity, learning, resilience, vitality.

Narrowed down to five: family, gratitude, integrity, learning, vitality.

Final three:

- Family

- Learning

- Vitality

Identifying your own values should give you a different way to look at your organization's values or mission statement. Do those values feel closer to your values, now that you know where you stand? Or are you simply waiting for the margarita cart on Friday? *Not that there's anything wrong with that. You do you.*

"I can think of times I was deeply unhappy at work and I was not able to make that work situation better," says Liz Pearce, the CEO of FreshChalk and former Googler, whom we will hear from throughout this book.[24] "In every case, I left that work situation. The fact that you're unhappy at work is a sign that something is wrong. And if there's not a values alignment, that's the breaking point."

Paolo, meanwhile, knows he's in the right place at the right time.

"REI makes people feel more welcome outdoors," he told me in 2020, "and in this moment [during the tumultuous years of COVID-19], the social benefits, the lifestyle benefits, equity, climate, race—our mission is more important and more tangible than ever."

CHAPTER 5

———

THE WORLD'S MOST EXCELLENT SHEEP

I think of courage like a muscle. When you have
your "why" in front of you, you can push through.
—STARLA SAMPACO

Back in the days before Facebook, before Twitter and TikTok and Instagram, blogging ruled the internet. Working for *The News Tribune* in Tacoma, Washington, my job was to help bring the newspaper's efforts online to reach new and changing audiences. At the time, however, most of the journalists I worked with were having trouble seeing how—or why—they would make time for this new form of publishing.

Mike Sando covered the Seattle Seahawks for the newspaper, and NFL Draft weekend was fast approaching. He came to me and said he wanted to publish online a separate story for each draft pick the Seahawks made during the two-day event. Of course, I jumped at the chance. I told Mike I would set him up with a blog, and he would be able to publish the stories himself. The dirty little secret here is that I didn't want to work all weekend and be the middleman for the half-dozen posts Mike wanted to write each day. Yeah, it sounds pretty lazy in retrospect, but sometimes innovation comes in strange forms.

Mike felt nervous about publishing directly to the audience, since newspaper journalists had always relied on an editor and a copy desk to double-check their work before it made it into the newspaper. I told him I'd be available if he ran into any tech problems, and his editor would read the posts as soon as he published them. It worked. On Monday we huddled in the newsroom, and I reported that the blog had received 16,000 page views over the weekend. "Is that good?" they asked. "Absolutely," I said. That was more traffic than any other news story on the website. We had also trounced the competition, as none of the bigger Seattle newspapers or TV stations had been publishing in real time, so rabid Seahawks fans had only had one place to turn if they didn't want to wait for the evening newscast or the next morning's newspaper.

I asked Mike to keep the blog going, and his first response was No—he didn't have time to maintain a blog in addition to his regular newspaper assignments. I convinced him to keep it going for one week, to cover the press conferences related to the players selected in the draft, and he agreed. As he continued to post, however, positive comments started showing up on the blog. "Great job, Mike!" "This blog is so awesome." "Keep up the good work." At the end of the week, Mike agreed to keep it going.

A couple years later, I joined the other senior editors in a meeting with Mike, who had just returned from a job interview with

ESPN. We were hoping to counter whatever offer he received and keep him at the newspaper, since he had become such a valuable player on our team. But ESPN had offered to double Mike's salary, let him work from home, and travel to cover any NFL game he chose each week. "Congratulations!" we said in response.

"Part of it is just being open to new ideas," says Mike, who joined *The Athletic* in 2019 after twelve years with ESPN.[25] He has voted on the Pro Football Hall of Fame every year for the past decade, and has covered every Super Bowl since the 1998 contest. "When I think back to what the job was and what were my career aspirations at the time? I guess I aspired to be a columnist, as it was the next step and up a pay grade. The actual next thing didn't exist when I got in the business. I'm fortunate you approached me. But I could have easily said, 'Oh, I have family stuff, my commute is too long, I've got this other stress; could we get someone else?'"

Mike Sando

This chapter will help you identify and act on opportunities that currently exist in your world. Growing, and finding more fulfillment, are essential to maximizing The Butterfly Impact for your work-life happiness. Not everyone can rise to the pinnacle of a career the way Mike Sando has, but we can all learn how to move beyond our comfort zone.

"You can always find a reason to not do something that is new," Mike told me. "When I look back, I can see how I limited myself so many times. And often you see a person who has great potential but settles for what they are currently doing. You can't even see it in yourself, because you've never been told to dream it. A lot of people don't know someone who took a chance."

Mike has taken plenty of chances during his career and discovered one innovation after another. Shortly after the blog took off, he started playing around with Excel to dive into the analytics of football games, years before that became an industry standard. He even tapped the blog's readers to help him construct the formulas that would automatically update the spreadsheet as he tracked plays in games. Eventually he needed a larger, more powerful computer to keep up.

"I try to always be looking for new ways and an edge. There's always a safer path, so I've been retraining my thinking: What if I got laid off? I could be having to reinvent myself, and the minute I got laid off I'd be gung ho, but behind. I could be doing three other things right now and not have to leave my job. And it could open up entire new avenues."

Today he's known to NFL fans and around the league for his annual QB Tiers analysis, which slots all NFL quarterbacks into one of five tiers based on interviews with fifty coaches and front-office personnel.

"It [QB] is the one position everyone watches," Mike says. "It takes months to put together. Lots of conversations. My goal has always been don't make it too overly complicated. I don't need five paragraphs to explain it. And people seem to enjoy it."

Sports writing has been done a certain way for a very long time (as someone who originally wanted to be a sportswriter, I should know). Looking back, it's no surprise to me that Mike's career has blossomed because of his ability to take initiative and reshape his job to meet—and often exceed—the expectations of his readers. *The Athletic*, where Mike works now, is a perfect fit. It quickly grew a subscription-based sports news service where readers pay a monthly fee for access to the best sports writing around. It's basically the Netflix of sports writing and analysis—a company that found a better way to serve sports fans the content they now can't live without.

INITIATIVE LEADS TO INNOVATION

Taking initiative in your job can be an absolute game-changer. Michael Housman led a project to figure out why some customer service reps stayed in their jobs longer than others. The study included data from over 30,000 employees who handled calls for banks, airlines, and cell-phone companies. Adam Grant, a professor at the Wharton School of Business and one of my favorite workplace-well-being geeks, wrote about the study in his book *Originals*.[26] The question Housman sought to answer: why did some customer service reps leave their jobs while others stayed?

The answer turned out to be tied to which web browser a person used. A customer service rep who used Firefox or Chrome remained in their job 15 percent longer than one who used Internet Explorer or Safari. But the advantage of using Firefox or Chrome wasn't technical; it was a matter of mindset.

"To get Firefox or Chrome, you have to demonstrate some resourcefulness and download a different browser," Adam Grant wrote. "Instead of accepting the default, you take a bit of initiative to seek out an option that might be better."

The employees who took the initiative to change their browsers to Firefox or Chrome approached their jobs differently. They looked for novel ways of selling to customers and addressing their concerns. When they encountered a situation they didn't like, they fixed it. Having taken the initiative to improve their circumstances, they had little reason to leave.

"We live in an Internet Explorer world," Grant added. "Just as almost two-thirds of the customer service reps used the default browser on their computers, many of us accept the defaults in our own lives."

 BUTTERFLY IMPACT SIGNPOST

"Don't wait to be anointed" is a saying I heard years ago and have repeated many times since in workshops, presentations, and conversations with various work groups. Whether you take initiative by discovering an entirely new and innovative way to do your job, or simply download a different web browser to your computer, the practice of looking for novel ways to do things is one of the best ways to activate The Butterfly Impact in your world.

It's up to you to make your job better, especially when you are looking to advance in your career. Why would someone trust you to run a team or a department if you can't create your own high-performing model, exceeding expectations and taking on more responsibility than what's in your job description? If you don't find ways to do your job better, faster, and with more validation, it won't change. Unfortunately, we have all been conditioned to stay in line and not rock the boat. Another study referenced in Grant's book focused on elementary school teachers who were asked to rate students on a list of characteristics. The least favorite students were the non-conformists who made up their own rules. It turns out teachers tend to discriminate against highly creative students.

"In response, many children quickly learn to get with the program, keeping their original ideas to themselves," Grant wrote, adding that, in the language of author William Deresiewicz, they become "the world's most excellent sheep."

People don't want to feel like sheep, no matter how excellent sheep might be. The formal term among researchers for taking initiative in your job is *job crafting*. And it has many positive effects, including increased engagement in your work and the satisfaction of learning new skills or approaches. Job crafting can be a powerful tool for reenergizing and reimagining your work-life which, of course, is the essence of The Butterfly Impact.

The challenge, of course, is getting the work done that you were hired to do while finding time for crafting your job: prioritizing the tasks and the people that make the work more fulfilling to you. The goal is to change your job gradually. Gradual change helps to avoid the painful process of approaching your manager and asking to re-write your job description, which would require the involvement of HR and your boss's boss, adding much unnecessary bureaucracy to the situation. This is precisely what holds back many people from the important work of job crafting: they wrongly assume that a manager needs to change their title or make a big announcement in order for them to find more meaning in their work.

That's not to say that you want to keep your manager or teammates in the dark. Ideally, you can work with them to develop your future state. To foster support for your job crafting, focus on creating value for others, building trust, and identifying the people who will support you. You can maximize The Butterfly Impact by inspiring your teammates to try the process, too. Just think how much better your work life can be if everyone around you is maximizing their own motivations, strengths, and passions, too.

COURAGE IS LIKE A MUSCLE

It takes ambition to take initiative over your job or career, something Starla Sampaco knows well. I hired Starla as an intern in 2017, impressed with the poise and professionalism she displayed, especially at a relatively young age. A couple years later, Starla launched a YouTube channel, *Career Survival Guide*, to help professional women of color advocate for themselves at work. Consistent with that, she is following her passion and doing her own job crafting while also helping others find their path and overcome challenges.

"Women and people of color face unique barriers to professional success. No one prepares you for that, so I thought I could create the resources I wished I had," she told me.[27] "I tell people to think of me as the older cousin you would turn to for advice."

Starla Sampaco

One of the barriers Starla has fought to overcome with *Career Survival Guide* is the unfortunate response that, she says, women of color who are creators face when they publish online, especially when the content is related to issues of diversity and inclusion. It has taken courage for her to embrace the uncertainty of trying to build an audience from scratch, as well as the fear of what will be posted to her creative output.

"It can be scary. Woman-of-color creators have had horrible things said to them, and anytime I post about D&I, I can expect weird comments," Starla told me.

With courage, she's been able to manage the fear of online harassment with the fear of failure that every entrepreneur or artist feels when they start putting their work out into the world—all while creating a job that she loves, while also getting the satisfaction of helping others do the same.

"I think of courage like a muscle," Starla says. "When you have your 'why' in front of you, you can push through. Some days it does feel defeating. Those things can really crush you, especially if your work is personal. I just try to settle myself down and tell myself that, every day, I'm one percent closer to my goals."

If feeling incompetent on the job causes despair, then the opposite is also true: you are happiest when you are doing something you're good at. In fact, it can help you transform what feels like just a job into a true calling. This is a great way to activate The Butterfly Impact, too; as your work becomes more meaningful, you will have more positive energy for the rest of your life.

PLAY TO YOUR STRENGTHS

The first step in taking initiative is identifying your Signature Strengths, which were developed by Martin Seligman in his book *Authentic Happiness*.[28] Seligman, at the University of Pennsylvania, is a pioneer in the field of positive psychology. He and his colleagues used a rigorous process to develop a list of twenty-four character strengths. Examples include curiosity, kindness, love of learning, and social intelligence. This became the basis for a personality test that you can take to determine your Signature Strengths. Think of the Signature Strengths as those that are the most essential to who you are. They come to you most naturally, so you can also leverage them relatively easily; that makes them more important than other character strengths.

If you identify your Signature Strengths and put those strengths into action, Seligman suggests, you will feel like you're flourishing.

"What causes this is that you experience positive emotions in your job. Which makes you more productive. Which makes you like your job more and so on," Yale professor Laurie Santos says.[29] "Using your strengths and those positive experiences tends to contribute to you thinking your job is a calling."

If you use four of your Signature Strengths at work, that is the "sweet spot," according to Santos. It works for me. According to the VIA Survey of Character Strengths, my top four Signature Strengths are:

- Curiosity and interest in the world

- Citizenship, teamwork, and loyalty

- Love of learning

- Zest, enthusiasm, and energy

To give you a sense of how this looks in real life, consider this project from my work: in 2017, shortly after starting my consulting role, I came up with a concept called IdeaLab; the goal was to build a culture of innovation among eight ABC-owned TV stations around the United States. With help from many other people, most notably my colleagues Anna Robertson and Jason Potts, it has grown into a meaningful and influential component of the organization. Here's how it aligns with my character strengths:

1. **Curiosity and interest in the world.** To produce the original concept, I researched how other organizations structured internal innovation programs.

2. **Citizenship, teamwork, and loyalty.** To get it off the ground, I worked with a small group of stakeholders in the corporate office to move the idea forward. Then we selected a "champion" at each of the eight TV stations to collaborate and drive awareness locally.

3. **Love of learning.** I researched and identified a new software platform to easily capture and organize the ideas. I learned how to use the tool through sessions with the software company that built it, then taught others.

4. **Zest, enthusiasm, and energy.** I have continued to evangelize the program on group calls and in-person during station visits. The program has evolved greatly over the past three years, thanks to the help of many other stakeholders who share my enthusiasm for it.

Hundreds of ideas have been submitted, and the monthly showcase connects more than 150 people across the country to feature and discuss the best experiments from that month. I've seen presenters overflow with pride as they talk about projects that are obviously high points of their work careers.

After each of those monthly calls, I feel like I'm flourishing. And my job feels like a calling, in that I was the right person for this job at this time.

My original career plan was a bit different. I wanted to be a high school football coach. Looking at my Signature Strengths today, I can see how they would apply to coaching football as well as they do to management consulting. Getting to know a new group of players each year would serve curiosity and interest in the world; teamwork would obviously be integral to the ultimate team sport; I would have to constantly be learning new strategies for offense and defense and how to motivate teenagers; and if any occupation is a picture of "zest, enthusiasm, and energy," it's that of a high school football coach.

"Find a job that you love, and you'll never work another day in your life." A legendary high school basketball coach named Ed Pepple told me that during an interview over coffee and pancakes one weekday morning in 1997. As a newspaper reporter covering high school sports at the time, I took copious notes about everything else he said that day, but that's the only thing I remember.

Our culture tends to put the focus on "finding" the right job, as if once the search ends and "the job" is found, life goes on cruise control and you ride off into the sunset. It's similar to the Hollywood rom-com fantasy that tells us finding the right person is the happy ending to the story when, in fact, anyone who has been in a relationship knows that's when the work actually begins. "Happily ever after" is, indeed, just a fairy tale.

MAKING IT HAPPEN

The best times in life happen when the best of you is brought to life. Once you recognize the strengths that represent the best of you, it will be easier to integrate them and prioritize them in your work-life. Here's how to get started:

- **Identify your Signature Strengths.** Take the quiz at via-character.org.

- **Activate your Strengths.** Use one of your Strengths in a new and different way every day for one week.

- **Craft Your Job.** Intentionally prioritize tasks and activities that leverage your Signature Strengths. Talk to your manager about how this can help the team and organization achieve its goals.

The grass isn't always greener, of course. If you're having trouble finding your dream job, or your calling, take a moment to think through what it would take to feel purpose and enjoyment in your current job. You might be able to flourish where you work with a little effort and intention.

CHAPTER 6

WHEN THERE'S TOO MUCH WORK

If you want something done, ask a busy person.
—BENJAMIN FRANKLIN[30]

When the alarm sounded at 3 a.m., Michelle Li would crawl out of bed, keeping the room dark so her husband might remain asleep. In the bathroom, as she waited for the shower to warm, she would find her waterproof earbuds and open her iPhone to the podcast she had been listening to the day before, then get into the shower.

Michelle had to be ready for work by 5 a.m. every weekday for years—ready to appear on TV. As a morning reporter and anchor, she worked a full day before most people had their first break. By 10 a.m., she would be ready to resume her "other job" as mother to toddler J.J. She relieved her husband and spent the rest of the day trying to "sprinkle in work" when she could while keeping up with her son, and even finding time to nap with him in the afternoon.

"Toddlers are hard," Michelle told me.[31] "I know we'll never have this time again so it's been pretty cool, but sometimes I think: Can I just get a break please?"

Juggling all that life and work entail is challenging for most people, but even more so if you are like Michelle (or Shauna Causey or Kimmie Sakamoto). She's constantly looking for a new way to do her job, be a better mom, and take care of herself. She also has new ideas to pursue, like her financial podcast on managing your money (named *Monetary Li Speaking*), which she recorded multiple times a week while J.J. napped. She told me it's "impossible" to work full time *and* be a full-time mom, but she continues to try.

In March of 2021, Michelle and her family moved back home to Missouri. She said she would miss Seattle, but, following the death of her mother, "it was the only option that made sense." Instead of doing the morning news, she would be working for the late newscast. There wouldn't be any more 3 a.m. alarms because she would be moving to the opposite end of a normal schedule.

How do you balance everything, including the basic domestic demands of food and clean clothes?

"The first thing is to have grace with yourself," Michelle says. "I use a lot of shortcuts and I'm a huge list-maker. I schedule in everything, even picking up groceries. Everything."

Michelle Li

She also uses calendars—both a whiteboard calendar in her kitchen, and a Google calendar online. And timers. "I often set timers for myself: Do this for the next thirty minutes and then move on to the next thing."

Time management and organization are skills that some take for granted and others obsess over eternally. Some of us are born with the ability to juggle multiple tasks and assignments simultaneously, while others will always struggle with it. It's no secret that stress and anxiety are by-products of feeling that there's simply too much to do and not enough time. Yet our society has wrongly associated a person's relative state of busyness with their overall value (remember the "cult of busy"?). It's time to swing the pendulum back the other way, and value those among us who seem to always have time for a call, a coffee, or a happy-hour meet-up. Those who seem time affluent.

It's such an important factor in creating more work-life happiness that I am devoting multiple chapters to it. In this chapter we will focus on how to organize your life and make the most of your time, paying close attention to the mental and emotional impact that comes from feeling overwhelmed, which started simply enough with just being busy.

 **BUTTERFLY IMPACT SIGNPOST**

No matter how many items are on your to-do list today—or even if you have been too busy to make a list—it's important to address the emotional side before you can tackle the rational side and actually get things done. (Remember the Elephant and the Rider?) While it seems counterintuitive, adding to your list will actually help you manage it better. Attack the overwhelm and stress first. In the end, you'll be more productive.

As the saying goes, you have to make time to sharpen the saw, and in this case, the saw is you—body and mind.

One of the best ways to sharpen the saw is to move your body, even a little bit. Walk, jog, stretch, yoga, push-ups, dancing; almost any amount of exercise has been proven to enhance your mood and energize your ability to tackle that task list. Just a few minutes will change your perspective and bring balance between your emotional and rational selves.

"The link between exercise and mood is pretty strong," says Michael Otto, PhD, a professor of psychology at Boston University.[32] "Usually within five minutes after moderate exercise you get a mood-enhancement effect."

And a little bit can go a long way. Moderate-intensity aerobic exercise not only improves your mood immediately, but those improvements can last up to twelve hours, according to Dr. Jeremy Sibold.[33] Even moderate exercise has the potential to "mitigate the daily stress that results in your mood being disturbed."

As Andrew Solomon observed in his 2001 book, *The Noonday Demon*: "The opposite of depression is not happiness, but vitality."[34] Reams of evidence support the positive impacts of exercise on mood, stress, and anxiety relief. And a bonus: it burns calories, too.

Once you've reset your mood with a little movement, then what? The answer is systems and structure. David Allen, author *Getting Things Done*, has found that failing to "get things done" will sabotage your self-esteem.[35] His methodology and framework have helped millions of people for more than two decades, so he's clearly figured something out. While productivity is the end goal, clearing the mind of all those things that need to get done is the essential first step. "Your mind is for having ideas, not holding them," Allen says.

Allen's goal is to help people achieve "stress-free productivity." I love this because it tackles the stress and anxiety that ruins most people's work-life happiness, in addition to boosting productivity. Allen has built a cult-like following (who call themselves *GTDers*) with his book, podcasts, and public appearances. Here are a few of Allen's suggestions on where to start:

- **Write down what's on your mind.** Even if you take a mere three minutes and jot down the top-of-mind things rattling around in there, you're doing great.

- **Clean a drawer.** No kidding. It's one of the best therapies in the world for getting back in your psychological driver's seat.

- **Tackle one pile.** There's likely at least one stack of stuff somewhere in your environment that you've gone somewhat numb to, but you know it contains things to be sorted and organized—trashed, filed, or curated for next actions or projects.

"Cleaning makes everything better," says Liz Pearce, a serial CEO and former Googler.[36] "Clearing things away and making a calm space helps me clear my mind for work."

Pearce, a single mother with two children who has been leading fast-growth startup companies for more than a decade, doesn't subscribe to the "cult of busy." Incredibly, she says she doesn't feel short on time. She credits having "a lot of energy" and working hard to not let things build up, knowing that if she lets things build up, it's harder to get anything done.

That's where a system like Allen's can make a huge difference. When I first read *Getting Things Done* almost twenty years ago, I found it a bit overwhelming, so I cherry-picked a few parts of the system and tested them in my life. This has been my approach with most self-help, productivity, and healthy-living books: experiment with a few parts to see if they fit into my life and ignore the rest. As Bruce Lee once said, "Absorb what is useful, discard what is useless and add what is specifically your own."[37]

I've personally found it helpful to have a simple, repeatable process for jotting down or capturing everything that needs to get done; try it—it will make your life easier to manage. Pen on paper, a spreadsheet on your laptop, or an app on your smartphone, it doesn't matter how you convert the balls bouncing around your brain into artifacts, just as long as you do it. Often.

"Are you a list maker?" is a question I asked regularly when interviewing people for this book. There is a shared appreciation among list-makers for the relief in jotting down everything on their plate, and the pure joy in crossing items off the list as each task is completed. *Like many ardent list-makers, I've been known to add something to my list that I already completed just for the mini rush of accomplishment that I feel when crossing it off.*

The challenge is more than just how to be productive, of course, especially when it comes to more than cleaning out a drawer. In order to be successful in a job or career, it's important to be effective as well as productive. You can check off ten things on your to-do list, but if the single most important item on that list doesn't ever get done, you've failed.

"If you want something done, ask a busy person" is a quote by Benjamin Franklin. I remember hearing it in college at a point when I had a full course load of seventeen credits and three part-time jobs (I had an internship at the local daily newspaper, was managing editor of the college newspaper, and waited tables at a restaurant). I've always had at least one side project or second job. Whether it's writing a book, trying to build a smartphone app for food photography, or teaching a graduate-level course at the University of North Carolina, I've found the more I have to do, the more effective I am in everything I do. And I'm not alone.

"I think it's the power of cognitive variety," says Paolo Mattola from REI, who also teaches marketing classes at a community college and graduate school for the University of Washington.

"You get to see how different organizations work and that brings freshness to [your] day job."[38]

Whether it's work-life balance, work-life blending, or work-life happiness, the construct of only two things—work and life—doesn't work for people like Paolo. He seeks out and embraces additional challenges and opportunities, not because he wants to avoid his day job and his personal life, but as a way to make them more meaningful. This could be a hobby or passion project instead of another job: appearing in a community play, singing with the church choir, or coaching youth sports, for example. Or starting a podcast, as Michelle Li did, even though she clearly didn't have any "extra" time in her day.

"I need to break my own bubbles and create different bubbles," Paolo says. "It's more hours worked but it's more productive, because I shift gears into different perspectives. It's a polar thing and a way to add a vector. I've decided my emotional cognitive balance will tip over, so I've added a third wheel." What Paolo means here is that only focusing on work and family—two points of contact—makes him feel out of balance, like a bicycle that is not moving. Adding a "third wheel" creates balance and helps him continue growing as a person, creating new experiences, or "bubbles" as he calls them.

Wait, I know you're thinking, *You're suggesting that my overwhelming to-do list needs more things to do!?* Yes, I am, and there's more. You need to build in artificial buffers to your schedule for additional breathing room, if only to avoid falling prey to the *planning fallacy*. Have you ever underestimated how long a task will take, even if it's a task you've done before? We all have. That's the planning fallacy, and it can destroy any good to-do list and create additional stress and anxiety.

"One way to protect against this is simply to add a 50 percent buffer to the amount of time we estimate it will take to complete a task or project," Greg McKeown writes in *Essentialism*.[39] This could be adding blocks of time to your work calendar to separate the hour-long video calls and meetings, as LinkedIn CEO Jeff Weiner does. Or simply leaving fifteen minutes early to take your daughter to soccer practice when you "know" it will only take ten.

"Not only does this relieve the stress we feel about being late… but if we do find that the task was faster and easier to execute than we expected (though this is a rare experience for most of us), the extra time feels like a bonus," McKeown writes.

Weiner, who is likely busier than most of us, schedules two hours of blank space in his calendar every day. At first, it felt like an indulgence or a waste of time, he told McKeown. But eventually he found it to be his single most valuable productivity tool.

Another way to become less busy, or to tackle the task list that has spilled over onto the next page and now feels hopeless, is to scrutinize what is on that list, and how you are spending your time. This is simple but not easy. The practice should extend beyond your task list and fully encompass every other way you are spending your time, too. It's the crux of McKeown's book (subtitled *The Disciplined Pursuit of Less*).

In his 2009 book *Anything You Want*, Derek Sivers conveyed similar advice more bluntly: "If you're not saying, 'HELL YEAH!' about something, say 'no.' Use this rule if you're often over-committed, or too scattered. When deciding whether to do something, if you feel anything less than 'Wow! That would be amazing! Absolutely! Hell yeah!'—then say 'no.'"

Sivers is one of my favorite thinkers. He writes constantly, appears on countless podcasts and is one of the most generous people with his time I've met (even replying to my emails about opinions from my teenage son about the philosophy of art.) Most of us didn't grow and sell an online music company for $22 million like Sivers, so we may not have *quite* the freedom he does, but you can apply his approach to more common work-life puzzles.

A related method offered by McKeown is the 90 percent rule: as you evaluate decisions or dilemmas you're currently facing, give each one a score from 0–100. If you rate any lower than 90, automatically change its score to 0 and simply reject it.

If numbers aren't your thing, think of how organizational guru Marie Kondo would look at your task list: if it doesn't bring you joy, get rid of it. "Right now, my work sparks joy, but there was a time when my schedule was so packed, I was physically and mentally exhausted," Kondo writes in *Joy at Work: Organizing Your Professional Life*. The 2020 book with co-author Scott Sonenshein is a work-targeted extension of the ground-breaking approach she popularized in *The Life-Changing Magic of Tidying Up*, which sold millions of copies worldwide.[40]

The bigger challenge, of course, is what to do if it's your boss who's asking you to do something that doesn't give you joy, score ninety points on an imaginary scale, or make you say, "HELL YEAH!" This is where building a healthy relationship with your boss really pays off. Explain the trade-offs with your time if you take on that new project or task that he or she just assigned you. What will it replace? Which is more important? Will it make your boss say, "HELL YEAH!"? Or bring him or her joy?

Time is a zero-sum game. You can't make more of it, so you

have to exchange one task, one hour, for another. Here are a few ways to make the most of yours.

MAKING IT HAPPEN

- At work, be disciplined about how you evaluate your time and your calendar. Kondo's *Joy at Work* co-author Scott Sonenshein offers this three-question test:

  ○ Is this task required for me to keep—and excel at—my job?

  ○ Will this task help create a more joyful future, for example, by helping earn a raise, get a promotion, or learn a new skill?

  ○ Does this task contribute to more satisfaction at work?

- "Your task pile is like a mirror—it reflects what you're currently doing," Sonenshein writes. "How do you feel when you look in the mirror?"

- Color-code your calendar. This makes it easy to evaluate at a glance where you're planning to spend your time. If that high-priority project is color-coded red and you don't see many red blocks on your calendar for the week, your time and your priorities do not align.

- For your hours away from the job, create a time portfolio. Just as you want a diversified financial portfolio to reflect your short- and long-term goals, how you spend your time outside of work should reflect your priorities and your values.

- What activities help you recharge and sharpen the saw? Is there enough time for that on the weekend? (Or any time for that?)

- What percentage of time is spent doing things you want to do, compared to things you feel you have to do? It could be something fun, frivolous, or trying something new like a recipe or restaurant. You need to schedule time for yourself, too.

- How much time do you protect for nothing? Just like the LinkedIn CEO schedules blank space in his workday calendar, you need to schedule blank space into your off-hours for curiosity, serendipity, and rest.

- The challenge of managing email can be daunting all by itself. One of my favorite tips from Allen's GTD system is "the two-minute rule": if you can deal with an email in two minutes or less, do it now.[41] Create as many folders for saving emails as you need to keep your inbox relatively clean. Create one folder for "waiting for information" as a temporary container to hold those emails that are waiting for a response and keep them away from your consciousness.

The pursuit of time affluence may appear selfish, but the more time you have for yourself, the more time you can give to others, as well.

As Michelle reminded us at the beginning of this chapter, give yourself some grace. Take time to sharpen the saw. Then use it on the things that matter most.

CHAPTER 7

SECRETS TO BE ORGANIZED IN WORK AND LIFE

If you want to change the world, start off by making your bed.

—NAVAL ADMIRAL WILLIAM MCRAVEN

If you could make someone's dream come true, wouldn't you want to do it as often as possible? Julie Swenson is a ray of sunshine always on the lookout for a nugget of inspiration to share and a dream to make real. She works in the mortgage industry, a world filled with shifting interest rates, endless forms to sign, and loads of financial pressure. Julie sees her industry as fulfilling the dreams of her clients.

"People laugh at my pipeline report—it's huge!" Julie says with a chuckle, even though she often works weekends, processing approval letters for her clients to take with them as they shop for their new home.[42] "I take it personally. I get affected because I look at [clients] like my family. Some people just do it as a job."

She works countless hours each week, often waking up before 4 a.m. In researching the best practices of productivity and personal organization for this chapter, one concept became clear to me: finding the hours of each day that are the most valuable for you is the key to being organized at work and in life. Whether you're a morning person or a night owl, identify and protect your window for getting that edge. Once meetings, emails, and the other pressures of life begin pulling you in multiple directions, productivity plummets.

"We do more before 9 a.m. than most people do all day," bragged a memorable US Army ad campaign in the 1980s. Julie follows a similar approach: Win By Noon is a program developed by Todd Bookspan specifically for loan officers and real estate agents. The program's workbook helps Julie plan and prioritize the most critical items on her to-do list each day. As the name implies, the goal is to complete the most important tasks by 12 p.m.

"That practice has really helped form me into a business," says Julie. To "win by noon" is only a part of the story of how Julie managed to break out on her own to become an independent mortgage broker in 2020, a time when her client load hit an all-time high. Daily, hours before she opens the Win By Noon workbook, she takes time to invest in herself.

Julie Swenson

Some days she's in her car by 4 a.m., driving to the gym some forty-five minutes away to meet her personal trainer. (Julie lives on a lake in the woods.) Others, she starts her day with coffee, a centering thought, a mantra, and an inspirational quote. In her journal, she captures something to be grateful for, her daily affirmations, and "today will be great because…" "Sometimes," Julie says, "it's just '…because I'm going to smile.'"

"Focusing my mind in the morning, it just helps me get better," Julie told me. "It really has changed my life."

Part of Julie's morning routine (and mine) comes from *The Miracle Morning: The Not-So-Obvious Secret Guaranteed to Transform Your Life by 8 a.m.* Originally published in 2012, Hal Elrod's book has been translated into thirty-seven languages, edited to target different occupations, and sold millions of copies.[43] The book series comprises titles specific to certain professions, such as *The Miracle Morning for Writers* and *The*

Miracle Morning for Salespeople. The morning ritual, including time for introspection, helped Julie form a personal mission statement that I happen to love: "To influence and inspire others to live a great story and pursue their spectacular." It goes far beyond finding the lowest rate on a thirty-year fixed.

 **BUTTERFLY IMPACT SIGNPOST**

If you don't make time to take care of yourself first, you won't be able to take care of everything, and everyone, on your list. It's just that simple. Some people love to be awake with purpose at 2 a.m. I prefer to go to bed early and wake up at 6 a.m. to start my routine. You can still have a "miracle morning" without getting up at 4 a.m., like Julie does.

Movie stars, pro athletes, billionaire investors, and four-star generals all seem to have one thing in common: mornings. Tim Ferriss, the bestselling author of several books, including *The 4-Hour Workweek,* has interviewed more than 200 "world-class performers" for his podcast, *The Tim Ferriss Show.* Several commonalities have emerged: *Start your day with time to think. Include a positive message. Move your body.* It's proven to help organize your day and focus on what's most important.

Given the extremes that Ferriss is known for, I was surprised to learn that his personal morning ritual is about as non-radical and safe as it gets. His list might surprise you:

1. Make your bed

2. Meditate

3. Hang (or exercise)

4. Drink tea

5. Journal

"If you want to change the world, start off by making your bed," says Naval Admiral William McRaven.[44] The reason that making your bed is so powerful is that it gives you a feeling of accomplishment first thing in the morning. McRaven explained it best during a commencement speech he delivered at the University of Texas: "If you make your bed every morning, you will have accomplished the first task of the day. It will give you a small sense of pride, and it will encourage you to do another task and another and another. By the end of the day, that one task completed will have turned into many tasks completed."

Bed makers are also more likely to enjoy their jobs, own a home, exercise regularly, and feel well rested, according to one study with 68,000 participants. Non-bed makers tend to hate their jobs, avoid the gym, and wake up tired. "All in all, bed makers are happier and more successful than their rumple-sheeted peers," Judy Dutton wrote in *Psychology Today*.[45]

I pulled up the covers on my bed this morning, as I do every day. I'd like to think that I would qualify as a bed maker for that study, but also guess that Admiral McRaven would be unimpressed with my attention to detail.

Once you've made your bed, carve out some time to think: About what you want to accomplish today. What you value. What you are personally building toward. And while you're at it, write it down. Then repeat.

"The brain doesn't distinguish between an experience that is intensely imagined and an experience that is real," according to James Doty, a clinical professor of neurosurgery at Stanford University. "Another mystery of the brain is that it will always choose what is familiar over what is unfamiliar. By visualizing our own success, I was making this success familiar to my brain."

Sounds like magic, right? It's actually science. Doty wrote about both in his 2016 book *Into the Magic Shop: A Neurosurgeon's Quest to Discover the Mysteries of the Brain and the Secrets of the Heart,* chronicling his life growing up poor with an alcoholic father and a chronically depressed mother. When Doty was twelve, he wandered into a magic shop and met a woman named Ruth, who taught him a series of exercises—including daily intentions—that he credits with changing his life and manifesting his success.

We are all equipped with *neuroplasticity,* the brain's ability to change and adapt to new inputs. Setting intentions every morning works because of something called the reticular activating system (RAS), which creates a filter for what you said you wanted to focus on and draws your attention toward it.[46] Have you ever thought about buying a new car and noticed that the make and model you're hoping to buy suddenly appears everywhere you look? That's your RAS. We are constantly bombarded by incoming information and competing thoughts throughout the day. Your RAS sifts through all the traffic in your head and helps you find the right lane to travel in toward your goal or intention.

"Most superheroes are nothing of the sort," Tim Ferriss wrote in another book, *Tools of Titans: The Tactics, Routines, and Habits of Billionaires, Icons, and World-Class Performers.*[47] "They're weird, neurotic creatures who do big things DESPITE lots of self-defeating habits and self-talk." Filling your brain with positive messages first thing in the morning will help counter that self-defeating chatter in your head. Ferriss says that 80 percent of the "world-class performers" he has interviewed have some sort of mindfulness or regular meditation practice.

Ferriss adds that if he has ten important things to do in a day, "it's 100 percent certain nothing important will get done that day." Which brings us to the next pillar of an organized work life: lists.

While there are many types of lists, let's focus on just two: task lists and checklists. I love lists of all kinds: grocery lists, bucket lists, brainstorming lists (for example, movies from my childhood I think my kids should see), but task lists and checklists will make the biggest impact on how you organize your work life.

Organizing Work and Life

A checklist, of course, is a set of repeatable steps to complete a process with all the given knowledge and information available. Atul Gawande traced the birth of the checklist to a flight competition in 1935 in his *New York Times* bestselling book, *The Checklist Manifesto.*[48] After a Boeing Model 299 crashed, killing two of the five crew members, a new approach to flying such a large, complex aircraft was needed.

Pilot error, it was determined, caused the crash. The new Boeing model was "too much airplane for one man to fly," according to one newspaper at the time. Test pilots then created a simple list, short enough to fit on an index card, with step-by-step checks for takeoff, flight, landing, and taxiing. "With the checklist in hand, the pilots went on to fly the Model 299 a total of 1.8 million miles without one accident," Gawande wrote. The army ultimately ordered almost 13,000 of them, which it named the B-17. Since flying the behemoth safely and reliably became possible, "the army gained a decisive air advantage in the Second World War, enabling its devastating bombing campaign across Nazi Germany."

Gawande goes on to explain how many professions—software engineers, financial managers, firefighters, police officers, lawyers—have become "too much airplane for one person to fly." Juggling the modern demands of work and life have, too. Your list of "things to do" today might have several items on it, but do all of them include the step-by-step directions of how best to complete that task? The best example of this, for me anyway, is seeing "groceries" on my task list and heading to the store without a specific list of items to buy or even a vague idea of what dinners I'll be making for my kids this week. You know the feeling, right? It's no different than having a morning ritual, a thirty-minute break for exercise, or time carved out for a side project without a plan. Or preferably, a checklist.

If checklists can dramatically decrease the rate of unnecessary deaths in hospitals around the world, as Gawande's book illustrates with numerous examples, think of how impactful they can be in your life. Checklists, Gawande writes, make up for "our inevitable human inadequacies" and bring simplicity to our increasingly more complex lives.

Lists, in general, are a proven way to develop a system for productivity and progress, to move toward what you want to accomplish in work—and life. Systems, not goals, are how change happens.

LISTS, IN GENERAL, ARE A PROVEN WAY TO DEVELOP A SYSTEM FOR PRODUCTIVITY AND PROGRESS, TO MOVE TOWARD WHAT YOU WANT TO ACCOMPLISH IN WORK—AND LIFE. SYSTEMS, NOT GOALS, ARE HOW CHANGE HAPPENS.

"To put it bluntly, goals are for losers," Dilbert creator Scott Adams wrote in *How to Fail at Almost Everything and Still Win Big*.[49] "Systems people succeed every time they apply their system, in the sense that they did what they intended to do. The goals people are fighting the feeling of discouragement at each turn. The systems people are feeling good every time they apply their system. That's a big difference in terms of maintaining your personal energy in the right direction."

In the previous chapter, Michelle Li showed us how she uses lists, calendars, and even timers to get everything done in her life, even recording a podcast while her toddler son naps. That's her system. David Allen's *Getting Things Done* approach is a system. *The Miracle Morning* is a system. Think of it like hiking a steep trail to the top of a mountain: each step is part of the process—the system—that takes you closer to your goal of reaching the summit and a scenic vista. You can't reach the top, or achieve your goal, with any of the individual steps. It takes all of them, one at a time, to reach the top.

My personal approach to managing my work life is a curated collection of several parts of disparate systems, and yours should be, too. I continually encounter new ideas and new approaches. Some I think are just interesting, but not worth trying. Others I try as a short-term experiment; if it feels like it's helping me, I add it. I may have to discard something else to make room, but that's the process of constantly refining your system so that it evolves and adapts as you do.

That's the secret to an organized work life.

MAKING IT HAPPEN

- **Establish or review your morning routine—with a checklist:** Wake up at least one hour before you need to be on a computer. ("Email is the mind-killer," according to Ferriss.) In a perfect world, what would you do with that time? Breathing exercises, body movement, and reading are all good options.

  During the dark winter months in the Pacific Northwest, I do a lot to create "hygge," a Danish and Norwegian word for coziness and comfort. A candle, a blanket, my comfy couch, coffee, and a journal or a book offering new ideas for life and work make up my go-to morning routine when I wake up before the sun.

- **Start or optimize your list-making:** There is no one-size-fits-all approach to lists. Take a few minutes to think about your list or lists, and evaluate whether the way you're doing them is working, or could be improved.

I keep several task lists going at once, separating out the to-do list for my consulting job from a different one for all things related to being an author. I use a software tool called Asana for both (with different logins to keep things separated). This allows me to organize each of those lists with different sections and priorities without feeling overwhelmed. I also use a white legal pad for an ongoing task list of everything else I need to get done, like order a birthday gift or pay bills or run a specific errand or fix the leaky faucet. I use a separate app (Google Keep) on my phone for things I need to buy at the store; one list is for groceries, one is for Costco, one is for house things. This is also where I keep the list of movies my kids should see, since my phone is always with me and I never know when I will think of a new one to add.

- **Establish or refine your system:** How do you spend your time each day? Is it intentional, the way you wanted to spend it, or haphazard, and you're just flying by the seat of your pants? While you can't anticipate all the interruptions, wild cards, and curveballs you will encounter tomorrow, you can create a system that protects your priorities no matter what comes your way.

A calendar is the best way to carve out time until you establish your system in a way that it just becomes part of your life. Remember the "big rocks exercise" from Stephen Covey in Chapter 1? Prioritize your "big rocks" every day so they will fit into your "jar."

For me, health is a big rock that must go in the jar first. That means making time to move my body every day, a protein smoothie for breakfast, and plants and protein for lunch.

Another big rock is cooking and eating dinner with my kids.

I fit these big rocks around the calls and meetings and dead-lines I have from my consulting job, and usually there's room for everything if I start my day early enough. When the work calendar is too full to accommodate everything else, I give myself some grace, and tell myself I will make it all happen the next day. It's a system, after all, and repeats every day.

It might sound trivial to include the smoothie, lunch, and dinner, but I know too many people who make food an option, something they do "when time allows." Person-ally, I know that this will lead me to ruin: low blood sugar, depleted energy, increased anxiety, and feeling "hangry" are a recipe for personal dysfunction for me, preventing me from getting things done (and doing a good job). So, healthy food and nourishment are part of my system. And family dinners have always been a priority, something I learned from my parents growing up.

* * *

Julie Swenson has a system. Years ago, while working in a downtown office, her system included writing a message of inspiration each morning on a whiteboard in the hallway out-side her office to share with passersby. As time went on, no one said much about her whiteboard messages, so one day she stopped. *Does anybody even care?* she thought.

A few days later, a man walked into her office and asked if she was the person who had been writing the positive messages. He told her it was hard to get to his office without something positive to inspire him. Julie then heard from the postal carrier, who snapped a photo of the message every day and sent it to his children. She started writing the daily messages again, and then started posting them on social media.

"Some of my friends were making fun of me, so I stopped doing it for a while," Julie says. She added that "it is amazing how many people told me, I need this in my life."

It's your system, and if it works, that's all that matters. If your system can help others and become part of their system, even better.

CHAPTER 8

DO WHAT YOU LOVE AND DO IT OFTEN

Here, I get a healthy specimen who I can treat without medicine. They leave here a happier person inside.

—APRIL COBLE

This chapter begins with a longer story, but it's worth it. It's about April Coble, who grew up in a family that loves water skiing. How much? When she was a baby, April's father carried her in his arms on a single ski along the Intercoastal Waterway in North Carolina. Her mother was a national champion, and, by the time April won her first national championship at age twelve, the sport had become the cornerstone of the Coble family.

In 1994, the family lost the lease on a house next to a perfect lake for their passion and desperately searched for a new place to call home. At the time, April was finishing pre-med studies and a biology degree in college, yet still "chasing buoys." She remained driven to keep improving at the family sport while competing on a national and, eventually, global stage.

April's parents placed a classified ad in *WaterSki Magazine* as part of an exhaustive search for a new place to call home that would accommodate their passion for water skiing. Eventually, the family connected with the owner of 170 acres about an hour south of Raleigh, North Carolina. April's father saw opportunity, even though the land was rough. After decades of strip mining, a series of half-mile-long, narrow, and shallow pits could barely be seen through the overgrown trees and brush.

The land had been untouched for twenty years, thanks to the Environmental Protection Act of 1974, and had been healing from all the years of mining. Over time, those pits had filled naturally with rainwater to become lakes. Perfect for water skiing. April's parents started clearing the land and setting up accommodations in a mobile home trailer, with a long-term vision of building a school where they could teach others the joy, skills, and technique of their beloved sport. April came home from college with a difficult decision to make: follow her academic path to medical school, or keep skiing and start teaching others what she had learned.

"I thought it was a temporary situation," says April, who agreed to give her family a year at home before continuing on.[50] "I was always torn because, while I was in school, everyone else was training year-round. And I had never been able to give a full-year commitment."

You've probably never heard of April Coble until now, yet she's one of the most accomplished athletes in the world. A thirty-time national champion, world champion, and Hall of Famer, she's succeeded at every level in the sport.

April Coble doing what she loves.[51]

"How did I get hooked? You have to have a competitive nature," April says. "When I was five, I got second place and I was upset that my trophy wasn't as big as the girl who won."

The championships—and the trophies—are not the best part of her decision to forego medical school for a life on the seven family lakes in North Carolina. The Coble family started teaching others to ski that summer in 1995, and more than two decades later is still going strong. I visited in October 2020 and fell in love with how the camp felt like family, even for a first-timer like me. At one point, as I was hanging out with the other campers, waiting for my turn to ski, I watched April's mom drive her decked-out golf cart down to one of the lakes and walk to the edge of a dock. April floated in on one of the brand-new MasterCraft ski boats after helping train a student. Her mom had important news: "I put the chicken in, and I think we have everything else we need for lunch," one national champion said to the other, in a sweet Southern drawl.

"Does money really make us happier?" asks Yale professor Laurie Santos. "The answer is: maybe a little bit."[52]

Santos would know. Her course Psychology and the Good Life has been called "the most popular class in Yale history." As the pandemic-related quarantine took hold in spring 2020, she offered a version of her Yale course online for free. I registered and joined more than three million people around the world. *Partly just so I can say I took a course at Yale.*

According to an often-cited Princeton study from 2010 that Santos uses in the course,[53] in the United States, most people showed increasing levels of happiness and emotional well-being until they hit an annual salary of $75,000. Then it plateaus and holds, even as a person's salary continues to rise.[54]

"Maybe if you're in the US and you only earn 10K a year, more money would make you happy. But for most of us, it's not going to make that much of a difference, and it's making way less of a difference than we actually think," Santos said.

April Coble could be the poster child for this research, since there isn't much money in competitive water skiing. April's original world tour took her to thirty stops, including fifteen outside of the United States. She made $20,000 in prize money, but it cost her $21,000 for the travel.

Money has never been the driver for the Coble family. April says the family couldn't afford the first land purchase in 1994, which they've added to over the years, but somehow her father found a way.

"I never saw it as a forever job," April said, twenty-six years after making the decision in 1995 to give it a year. "The land was so much work, we couldn't see an end in sight. As I reflect on what we've done, I'm super grateful for my dad's foresight. There's so much heart and soul poured into this place."

Instructors at the school don't get paid. They spend their vacation time working at the camp, helping others learn a sport they love. When April looks back on how differently her life path developed as a water-ski champion, coach, trainer, school administrator, and camp mom from what it would have as a doctor or dentist, she is both surprised and humbled.

"I'm just teaching people my passion, and a very difficult sport, I might add," says April, who helped me see that I actually knew very little about how to water ski, even though I'd been doing it for thirty years. "It's a feeling of such an accomplishment, especially the first time. The feeling is priceless."

This is your life. Do what you love and do it often.
—FROM THE HOLSTEE MANIFESTO

Sometime around 2011, I stumbled across the Holstee Manifesto online, and immediately ordered a print I could hang on my living room wall. It's helped inspire me to start companies (that failed—oh well), write books, and guide my life toward professional and personal fulfillment. Meeting April Coble and her family, I recognized that they are the living embodiment of this.

The story of the manifesto is almost as good as what it says.

Mike and Dave Radparvar teamed up with their friend Fabian Pfortmüller, and started planning to quit their jobs and follow their dreams of launching a new company to make and sell sustainable T-shirts and other goods. They met on the steps of Union Square in New York City in 2009 and, together, they defined what success would look like if they took the financials out of it.

The result, originally meant as a mission statement to guide them in creating a company that aligned with their personal values, became their best-selling product for many years. It has been viewed more than 50 million times, translated into fourteen languages, and called the next "Just Do It" slogan (which was popularized by Nike). The difference, according to University of Michigan marketing professor Scott Rick, is that Holstee explained what the "it" is.[55]

"'Just do it' got people buying shoes, leaving bad marriages, asking people to prom," Rick said. "This company seems to be very credible and genuine, so it's a familiar message but from a more sincere source."

Mike Radparvar told me the original intent of the manifesto was only "loosely connected" to the company.[56] "We did it just for ourselves. Similar to now [2020], we were losing faith; who really has our interests at heart when it comes to work or a job?"

THIS IS YOUR LIFE.

DO WHAT YOU LOVE, AND DO IT OFTEN.

IF YOU DON'T LIKE SOMETHING, CHANGE IT.

IF YOU DON'T LIKE YOUR JOB, QUIT.

IF YOU DON'T HAVE ENOUGH TIME, STOP WATCHING TV.

IF YOU ARE LOOKING FOR THE LOVE OF YOUR LIFE, STOP;

THEY WILL BE WAITING FOR YOU WHEN YOU START DOING THINGS YOU LOVE.

STOP OVER ANALYZING, ALL EMOTIONS ARE BEAUTIFUL.

LIFE IS SIMPLE. WHEN YOU EAT, APPRECIATE EVERY LAST BITE.

OPEN YOUR MIND, ARMS, AND HEART TO NEW THINGS AND PEOPLE, WE ARE UNITED IN OUR DIFFERENCES.

ASK THE NEXT PERSON YOU SEE WHAT THEIR PASSION IS, AND SHARE YOUR INSPIRING DREAM WITH THEM.

TRAVEL OFTEN; GETTING LOST WILL HELP YOU FIND YOURSELF.

SOME OPPORTUNITIES ONLY COME ONCE, SEIZE THEM.

LIFE IS ABOUT THE PEOPLE YOU MEET, AND THE THINGS YOU CREATE WITH THEM SO GO OUT AND START CREATING.

LIFE IS SHORT. LIVE YOUR DREAM AND SHARE YOUR PASSION.

THE HOLSTEE MANIFESTO © 2009   HOLSTEE.COM   DESIGN BY RACHAEL BERESH

The Holstee Manifesto. Visit holstee.com to learn more.

It guided the partners in forming the company and in their personal lives, according to Mike. Meanwhile, the manifesto began to spread—friends would send photos of the poster hanging in public places, including a luxury hotel in Amsterdam—which drew a lot of people to Holstee, the company. The message resonated with people, which changed the way Mike and his partners thought about their fledgling company.

"What we realized is they weren't interested in T-shirts," Mike says. "But [instead,] what does it mean to live this philosophy?"

The company quickly pivoted away from selling apparel (it hasn't sold any T-shirts in almost ten years) and toward the goal of helping people with the concept of "living fully and living mindfully." Holstee has built a community over the past decade, selling a handful of products, such as reflection cards and pocket journals, to people who hope to make a positive impact on their world and the world around them. The company also offers a membership program; more than 1,000 people are paying monthly to be part of their movement.

It's quite a different company than originally envisioned. The manifesto doesn't mean you have to quit your job—although that is one of the lines, and exactly what Mike, Dave, and Fabian did—or buy hundreds of acres in North Carolina to open a water-ski camp. It means you should think more intentionally about how you spend your time and attention.

 **BUTTERFLY IMPACT SIGNPOST**

"Life is short. Live your dream and share your passion," the Holstee Manifesto advises. My passion is learning. That love of learning has driven the direction of my professional life more than any specific activity, whether starting companies, writing books, or finding my way into the world of consulting. As a result, most of my time each day is spent doing something I love, which not only creates work-life happiness but makes me a healthier person overall.

The opposite is quite ugly. The negative impacts of actually hating your job, according to extensive research, go well beyond the obvious. You can't sleep, you get frequent headaches, you are constantly on edge and always tired, you get sick more often, may have chronic stomach issues, and may even lose interest in sex.[57] *Do I have your attention yet?*

Our culture trains us to believe that people who love their jobs are the exception, not the norm. I remember being in grade school—when the idea of work or a job meant little—and the teacher asked the class to raise our hand if we thought our dad liked his job. (Those were the days when most moms didn't work outside the home, although my mom seemed to always have one job or another.) Most of the kids (including me) raised their hands, and then the teacher replied with an assignment: When your father gets home tonight, ask him if he would do his job even if he didn't get paid.

My dad worked for the US Forest Service for thirty-five years as a civil engineer, designing logging roads. Like a lot of people of his generation, he didn't spend time thinking about joy in his job, or work-life happiness; he took pride in working hard and supporting his family. He retired with 4,000 sick hours, because the only day he called out sick was the day his wisdom teeth were removed.

His dedication had more to do with his work ethic than workplace happiness, however. He had found his way to the forest service by following his desire to get out of Grangeville, Idaho, the tiny town he had grown up in. His dad owned and operated a creamery in town and expected my dad and his brother to follow in his footsteps and work there after high school. My dad found a summer job with the Forest Service, however, and then received an offer to move to Bozeman, Montana, to work for the agency part-time while attending Montana State College. He packed his 1961 Pontiac Ventura two-door coupe and, to his parents' dismay, drove off into his future. Shortly thereafter, he met my mom and they married, then moved to Coeur d'Alene, Idaho, where I was born. They still live there, and have been married for fifty-seven years now.

What is your passion, and how much time each day are you spending with it at work? Can you increase that? And decrease the time you're spending on things you don't love doing? We don't live in the era of lunch-pail and time-clock factory work any longer. You have the ability—I would argue, the responsibility—to spend more work hours doing what you love, and less doing what you loathe. The Butterfly Impact makes it a responsibility because your ability to show up healthy, engaged, and fulfilled for the rest of the people in your life is your real duty. Punching a clock is not.

If this sounds too selfish, consider the wider implications for our society. Jeffrey Pfeffer, a professor at Stanford's Graduate School of Business, detailed some chilling data in his book *Dying for a Paycheck*:[58] "In total, workplace environments in the United States may be responsible for 120,000 excess deaths per year," he writes. That makes workplaces the fifth leading cause of death in the United States, with a hefty price tag: an estimated $180 billion in additional healthcare expenses, which is approximately eight percent of total healthcare spending. Pfeffer writes that about half of these deaths and about $63 billion (about one-third of the excess costs) might be preventable with improved work environments, cultures, and management.

Today's workers face new health risks that include being laid off, not having health insurance, irregular work shifts, working more than forty hours weekly, confronting job insecurity, facing work-life conflicts, having little control over one's job and job environment, facing high job demands, having low levels of social support at work, and working in unfair situations.

It can feel daunting to think about: What if you don't know what you love? Worse, what if doing what you love won't pay the bills? The reality of work and life, of course, is that there is some basic amount of income we all need for food, housing, and transportation.

Research—and common sense—tells us that some level of compromise is necessary to find happiness. Comedian Chris Rock touched on this in his 2018 Netflix special *Tamborine*, recalling the experience of sitting with his daughter in an auditorium at high school orientation. He described the program as grown-ups on stage lying to children about the future.

"You can be anything you want to be," Rock said one vice principal offered. "Lady, why are you lying to these children? Maybe four of them can be anything they want to be. But the other 2,000 better learn how to weld. Tell the kids the truth. You can be anything you're good at, as long as they're hiring. And even then, it helps to know somebody."

It's funny, but true. Doing what you love for work may feel like an unreachable goal for you, but it doesn't have to be a zero-sum game in which you switch completely from your "day job" to a passion project and hope for the best. An effective approach to following your passion begins with identifying what you love doing, what fulfills your spirit, and makes time fly by. Look for opportunities to make at least some money to sustain your living, and start forming a plan. Here are some recommendations on how to get started.

MAKING IT HAPPEN

- **Focus on your strengths.** Revisit Chapter 5 and the survey to identify your Signature Strengths. Compare your strengths to your interests and prioritize how, if you had a magic wand to design your days, you would spend your time.

  "Identify the set of things that you love to do and that you do well," Adam Davidson wrote in *The Passion Economy*,[59] which I highly recommend as a guide for this process. "You don't need to be the best in the world at something. People often succeed because they have a set of various skills that don't normally go together."

- **Ask for directions.** In this vast, interconnected world, there exists someone who is doing that thing you wish you were doing. Find that person. Then learn how they do what they do, and how they got to where they are. If you can directly connect with that person, even better.

  "Most of us don't know what to do next," Derek Sivers wrote in his 2020 book *Your Music and People*.[60] "We know where we want to be, but we don't know how to get there. The solution is incredibly simple and effective. Work backwards. Just contact someone who's there and ask how to get there. Call the destination. Ask for directions."

- **Make a plan that makes you happy.** Visualize "the destination" in as much detail as possible, combine it with the "directions" from Step 2, then break it apart into the smallest possible pieces. As you know by now, making tiny changes, repeated day after day, is how you reshape your life. Your plan should lead you to incremental progress toward your goal—and bring you joy. Remember, this is about doing more of what you love and less of what you don't. (Plus, it will be easier to follow if you enjoy it.)

* * *

"There comes a time when you ought to start doing what you want," Warren Buffett once said.[61] "Take a job that you love. You will jump out of bed in the morning. I think you are out of your mind if you keep taking jobs that you don't like because you think it will look good on your resume. Isn't that a little like saving up sex for your old age?"

For April Coble and her family, it's never been about the job. And it's always been about more than water skiing. Through countless hours spent taming the land and tending to the boats, April and her husband Chris, their parents, and their kids have cultivated a global family that has grown over the years. They care deeply about the people who come to the camp, which is why instructors spend their vacations working at the camp without pay.

"I was interested in medical school because I was intrigued by how the human body worked, and I just wanted to help people get better," says April, who notes that some of the kids who come to camp only get one hug during the year—hers. "Here, I get a healthy specimen who I can treat without medicine. They leave here a happier person inside."

I know I did. Thanks, April.

CHAPTER 9

MORE PLAY, NOT LESS

*An amazing amount of hours, an incredible
amount of learning, and I loved every minute.*
—CHRIS STANDIFORD

My freshman year at Gonzaga University, I remember walking
down the hall in my dorm and poking my head into one room
after another, trying to find someone interested in going to the
basketball game that night. The game had already started, but I
wanted to go check it out. I didn't want to go alone. I played basketball in high school, and have loved the sport my whole life. (I
still enjoy playing in my fifties.) Given that the gym was a short
walk from the dorm and the tickets were free, it seemed like a
no-brainer to me. Yet only my friend Mike agreed to join me.

We entered midway through the first half and found seats in
the student section near half-court. I don't remember if the
Bulldogs won or lost that game, or even whom they played. It
was just something to do on a weeknight, other than stay in the
dorm and do homework or goof off with friends. *I did much
more of the latter than the former.*

This story would shock students at the school today. Thousands of them camp outside in the cold Northwest winter days and nights to score tickets to Gonzaga basketball games. The program has become one of the most successful and celebrated in the nation over the past twenty years. In February of this year, *Sports Illustrated* featured the Zags on the cover with a simple title: "The Program."

The story of Gonzaga's rise to college basketball prominence illustrates the motivational power of play, and of working at something because you love it. The culture developed around a mission to continuously "find new ways to be successful," and stands as a near-perfect example of The Butterfly Impact: small, incremental, and sustainable changes over time can make a big impact that causes a positive ripple effect beyond the work at hand.

"You're most likely to lose weight—or succeed in any other endeavor—when your motive is play," Lindsay McGregor and Neel Doshi wrote in *Primed to Perform*.[62] "Play occurs when you're engaging in an activity simply because you enjoy doing it. The work itself is its own reward."

The concept of play in our society is, of course, most commonly associated with children. McGregor and Doshi are trying to change that, by reframing what play can mean, even in business. "When you read early-learning research, you see experiment, learning, curiosity," Lindsay told me. "There is nothing in our language that means all those things."[63]

Chris Standiford has been along for the whole ride at Gonzaga. Chris and I graduated in the same class in 1991. The majority of my friends and I flocked to Seattle, or other bigger cities, to find work in the midst of a recession, yet Chris stayed in Spokane.

He began working part-time for the athletics department at Gonzaga, while taking classes in pursuit of a master's degree in sports administration. As the athletics program expanded, new roles were created in the department. Chris loved every new opportunity, and jumped at the chance to grow with the program. Through opportunity, effort, and enthusiasm, he ascended to the position of associate athletics director, the number-two position in the department.

"It feels like fate; sometimes a path just gets laid out in front of you," Chris says now.[64] "There were no forks in the road. One opportunity unfolded, and then the next one, and the next one."

The nation's college basketball fans first heard about Gonzaga in 1999—eight years after Chris and I graduated. The team made an improbable run in the national tournament that year, highlighted by a dramatic buzzer-beater against the University of Florida. If you know anything about March Madness, you know that every year, a couple small schools no one has ever heard of pull a seemingly impossible upset and are dubbed Cinderella for the year. Just like the fairy tale, the clock always strikes midnight. Only Gonzaga has found a way to return to the ball and make a splash every year.

"Two things stick out from the early years," Chris says about the 1990s, when the basketball program's foundation began taking shape. "One, how much work it was. An amazing amount of hours, an incredible amount of learning, and I loved every minute. It was never tiring, just invigorating."

That's the power of play at work. When people are motivated to work together toward a common goal because they love what they are doing, great things can happen.

"And we were tiny. As we grew, we added staff. Most of the positions I've held were new positions," Chris says. Those new positions weren't part of some master plan, however. The architects of the program, head coach Mark Few and athletic director Mike Roth, added one piece at a time, consistently honoring their North Star: "Find new ways to be successful."

Chris Standiford

"You give opportunities to those people you believe in. And the ones that fit in the culture so well," Chris told me in 2020. Then, in June 2021, Roth announced he would be retiring after twenty-four years at the helm, and Chris was named to succeed him as Athletic Director. "It underscores who we are as an institution. The dignity of the person, with respect for being part of the education process, character development, and all that comes with that."

That's the approach, according to Chris, that Gonzaga has taken to grow from being anonymous to among the best of the best. The longevity of the leadership is truly rare. Roth supervised me in my freshman-year work-study program. I played intramural basketball against Few, and had communications classes with his wife, Marcy. He could have easily moved on to a bigger school and made more money at any time. If you love what you do, and whom you do it with, you stay where you are.

The ripple effect of that success on the basketball court has dramatically changed the university. The year before that Florida game, university enrollment was lagging, creating a $1 million budget crisis that resulted in layoffs across campus. A year later, the incoming freshman class jumped from 500 to 700 students.[65] In 2020, Gonzaga welcomed a freshman class of more than 1,200 students. Admissions applications have tripled, while the school's annual budget has mushroomed from $72.7 million in 1999 to $283 million in 2017.

"Find new ways to be successful." It sounds simple but it's not easy, especially with consistency, every day, over the course of years or even decades. The best way to do that is with play.

 BUTTERFLY IMPACT SIGNPOST

While your job may not be in athletics and literally tied to games that others play, you still can "play the game of business," as Bob Chapman says, with his concept of TGIM.[66] Play motivates us better than anything else. It creates adaptability in people and teams. It fuels progress and performance. Unfortunately, it's often disregarded as frivolous and a waste of time, especially in a world still finding its feet after the pandemic.

McGregor and Doshi's framework is based on research of

dozens of companies and thousands of employees. The traditional motivations of emotional or economic pressure, or simply doing things the way they've always been done, were found to be negative (and indirect motivators). The bottom line: people are more adaptable and perform at a higher level, solving problems and creating new ideas, with the positive (direct) motivations of Play, Purpose, and Potential.

PLAY

- You have time, space, and encouragement to experiment and learn

- You solve problems yourself

PURPOSE

- You see that your work is important and meaningful

POTENTIAL

- Your work is actively linked with your personal goals

- You focus your time on your strengths rather than your weaknesses

I started teaching this framework, and the importance of play, to organizations in 2019. "This is not foosball tables and margarita machines," I'd explain. Then I'd ask people to think of a great day at work—the kind of day when you go home and tell your friend, partner, or spouse that you had an awesome day. How would you describe that day? What made it awesome? People would talk about overcoming a difficult challenge, great teamwork, problem-solving, and a sense of purpose. "It felt like you were at play, right?" I'd suggest. Nodding heads and smiles around the room would confirm what I already knew.

Tanya Andrews knows as much about play as anyone I've met. For more than twenty years, she's been the executive director for an organization promoting play. It started as a children's museum, places of play that can be found in most cities. Children's museums are bursting with energy. Kids run excitedly from one station to the next. Laughter and joy are everywhere. There are things to climb on, things to paint, water tables to splash in, and grown-up scenario-setters like cash registers, garden tools, and fake plastic food.

Meanwhile, the children are learning. Yes, this is a powerful form of early education. Just don't tell the kids.

"Name me anyone more curious, loving, compassionate, eager, energetic, and in the moment than a child," Tanya told me.[67] "Adults are tired, we're usually stressed about something (of our making) and are usually wanting what we don't have. We should be learning from them. Play is something you don't have to teach a child—they are pre-wired to do it; play is innate. We should all use play to get beyond where we are right now."

I still remember *feeling* my kids learning at the children's museum, where I first met Tanya fifteen years ago. I joined the board of directors a year later. I learned about the research supporting early education and "thrive by five" programs. It only confirmed the obvious to me. Reading *Primed to Perform* many years later, I had the same feeling: We perform better when we are engaged, energized, and feel like we are at play. We are born this way. Just because there isn't recess after lunch or a water table at work doesn't mean we shouldn't continue looking for ways to play in our work. *I'm still in favor of recess after lunch, by the way.*

As McGregor and Doshi wrote, the highest performing and most adaptable cultures are those with the highest "total motivation," meaning that people do what they do because of positive motivations (Play, Purpose, and Potential). They call this TOMO. When the pandemic hit in 2020, organizations with high TOMO were able to adapt more quickly.

I saw ample evidence that the work I did with those organizations around Play, Purpose, and Potential paid dividends for them in 2020. I saw people and teams move faster, with more purpose and more conviction, than ever before. Lindsay told me that she saw the same thing in the organizations that her firm has been helping, too, even during some of the most stressful times that people have encountered.

"When you look into burnout, organizations that found a lot of play and purpose, where work mattered more than ever, didn't see burnout as a problem," Lindsay told me. "And these are people with incredibly hard jobs with incredibly high stakes—they didn't have the problems of burnout that others experienced."

"Find new ways to be successful." The pandemic forced every organization to find new ways to simply survive. The organizations with TOMO already in their culture were able to do this more effectively. Here are some ways to increase the amount of TOMO in your own life.

- **See what happens.** Experimentation and trying new things are great ways to play. This is the magic of watching a four-year-old playing at a water table, getting splashed, and laughing because of something she did. Grown-ups can do this, too.

"My favorite times in life started with a 'see what happens' approach," Derek Sivers wrote in *Your Music, Your People,* in the context of the FCC's emergency broadcast message we've all heard: "This is only a test."

"It's actually impossible to fail if your only mission was to see what happens!"

- **Look again.** Whatever it is that's causing you stress and or stifling your happiness, look at it in a new way through the lens of Play, Purpose, Potential:

  ○ **Play:** Do I get to try something new? Am I learning something new? How can I experiment in a way that would make this fun?

  ○ **Purpose:** How is this tied to my values? To the organization's mission? Will it help my team (or me) achieve a goal that has been stated and is valued?

  ○ **Potential:** Could this lead to something bigger: more time to work on projects I really enjoy at work? More responsibility or a promotion down the road?

- **Can you make it a game?** Create a points system that will score the progress. Identify a prize to be won. Incentivize something that helps "gamify" the task.

"Gamification is turning a task into a game in order to motivate yourself to do it," according to Deep Patel in *Entrepreneur Magazine*.[68] "The beauty of gamification is that the difficulty of a task (or how dreary it may seem) can be offset if you feel rewarded for completing it."

Entire companies have been created to help you do this with software. If you don't want to learn a new program, though, simply track your progress on a spreadsheet or notebook.

* * *

When work feels like play, good things happen. Learning happens. Growth happens. Connection happens. Just as compound interest builds your financial investments over time, valuing play in your work and life will help you build something amazing, little by little.

"I'm extremely proud of what has transpired here," Chris says of his experience at Gonzaga. "It was an unbelievable amount of great timing on my part.

"I've reflected a lot on how much I've changed. I recognize my values have stayed the same, while my behaviors have changed. I've found (my values) are ingrained in everything I do."

Find new ways to be successful. It's so much easier to do when it feels like play.

PART 2

WORK IS A TEAM SPORT

CHAPTER 10

WELCOME TO THE JUNGLE

The thing that makes us love our jobs is not the work that we're doing, it's the way we feel when we go there.
—SIMON SINEK

In 2008, Bill Sullivan started Accents & Interiors, a home finishings company, with seven employees. Bill grew up in Alabama, and, even though he has lived on the West Coast for decades, he has retained that sweet, Southern drawl, and a healthy habit of frequently using your name when he speaks to you, as in "Mark, I'll tell you what…"

The home finishings industry is a tough place to work. The people turn over often. Customers come and go, as do the carpet installers and other journeymen who need to be hired to do the work. Developers, subcontractors, and homebuyers can be a challenging mix to deal with. Business as usual means one problem after another: The materials didn't arrive on time. The installer didn't show up for work. The homebuyers changed their minds on the color.

Determined to get the company culture right from the beginning, Bill sat in the front of the office, next to the receptionist, for Accents & Interiors' first few years. Each time an employee would return from a job and walk through the front door without a smile, he would turn them around and walk them back out to the parking lot and ask them to try again.

"It's too hard of a job to do with a shitty attitude," Bill told me.[69] He remembers helping his team find a positive attitude—at least temporarily—"hundreds of times," as the company grew to twenty people in two years. "They would go back outside and grit their teeth and come back in with a smile.

"I just think it's that important," Bill says. If this sounds harsh, understand that Bill's intent has always been to bring out the best in people. He coached his three sons on more than seventy youth sports teams in nineteen years, and is one of the most giving and supportive people I know. He made community service projects a priority for his company, including feeding the homeless on Thanksgiving and Giving Tree projects each Christmas. "We help the community and strengthen the bonds between our employees at the same time. To me, this is much better than writing a check and sticking it in the mail."

In the company's early days, Bill did every job that was needed, from forklift driver and garbage man to CFO. Now that Accents & Interiors has more than sixty employees, Bill, as company president, sees his role as "protecting the culture of the company." That is why he personally leads new-hire orientation sessions that take up to four hours.

"I'm neurotic about the way we start people," Bill says. "It's all about who we are and what we do. We have rules and policies to weed out the people who need rules and policies. If (new hires) come back with a different attitude than what they showed during interviews, that just doesn't fly. I've let people go two days after we hired them."

Bill Sullivan and friends

Bill graduated from Auburn University, where every student needs to learn "The Auburn Creed,"[70] and uses it with his new employees. It's part of a multi-slide presentation that guides employee orientation sessions during onboarding. He explains every line, what it means to him, and what it means to everyone in the company.

"I believe that this is a practical world and that I can count only on what I earn," the creed begins. "Therefore, I believe in work, hard work." The creed, written by Auburn football coach George Petrie in 1943, covers honesty and truthfulness; a sound mind, body, and spirit; and respect for others, too.

Bill and his brother, Pat, a football star who won the Heisman Trophy in 1971, both attended Auburn, where Bill shared classes with Bo Jackson. "Our goal is relationships," says Bill. "How does your culture allow those personalities who wouldn't otherwise click to come together?"

Welcoming someone new to an organization is incredibly important, but most companies don't have a leader as passionate about the process as my friend Bill. You know the drill: new person shows up, meets with HR, fills out forms, and learns about health benefits and the 401(k) plan. If things are going well, someone from IT sends an email with login credentials so the new hire can get access to a computer and the systems they'll need. Someone, with luck a supervisor or team leader, shows the new person to their workstation (bonus points if the break room and restrooms are included on the walk through the office).

And after that, then what?

Unfortunately, it's common for new employees to feel isolated and unsupported. One study found that roughly one-third of new hires look for a new job within their first six months on the job. Among millennials, that percentage is even higher, and it happens earlier. Twenty-three percent of new hires turn over before their first anniversary.

For those who stay, it takes about eight months to reach full productivity. Eight months! This is why the onboarding process should extend way beyond the first day, week, or month—and it's an issue that everyone needs to have a stake in. If you don't work in HR, you might not think it's your job to provide the care it takes to support new employees at your organization, but everyone can—and should!—play a part in this process.

In too many cases, the employee sits dazed and confused, questioning why he or she decided to take the job. The traditional onboarding process misses what's most critical and immediate: people need to be connected to the culture of the organization as quickly as possible. Most new-hire checklists don't include those items. And that's where you come in.

BUTTERFLY IMPACT SIGNPOST

Whether you are a hiring manager or not, you can make an impact on how people are welcomed to your team. The more you help the new hires on your team connect to your culture, the more successful your team will be, and the greater the Butterfly Impact you will trigger for everyone involved.

Orientation is not onboarding. Orientation means showing a new employee the logistics of the job. The goal of onboarding should be to help a new employee love their job as soon as possible. Since you already work there, you know what they need to know. Your role should be less about how to do the work or find the restroom, and more about the people, the culture, and the purpose of what you do. Think about the emotional side of working where you do, and communicate that first. The HR team or another manager will take care of logistics like ID badges, parking spots, computer logins, and how to fill out a timesheet every two weeks. You can help with the more important task of helping the new person understand the culture and the meaning of the work.

Orientation is about the how. Onboarding should focus on the why.

"I think there is space for how someone is onboarded—specifically, when a group of people help someone understand what it means to be on this team," Forrest Lindekens, a consultant who works with Lindsay McGregor and Neel Doshi, the authors of *Primed to Perform,* told me during a video call. "It can't just be top-down. Strong cultures do this naturally, but getting there is intentional."

"The thing that makes us love our jobs is not the work that we're doing, it's the way we feel when we go there," Simon Sinek told Bob Chapman for his book, *Everybody Matters.*[71] "We feel safe; we feel protected; we feel that someone wants us to achieve more and is giving us the opportunity to prove to them and to ourselves that we can do that."

In most of the places I've worked, either as an employee or consultant, the tradition remains the same: On a person's first day at a new job, they might get an email introduction to the entire staff or a call-out in an all-hands meeting. On their last day, there's probably cake, speeches, and maybe even an alcohol-fueled goodbye party after work. It makes sense, of course. We don't really know this new person on their first day, but when they leave, we will miss them, so we have a ritual to celebrate and wish them well.

What if you celebrated people on their first day, too? At one company where I worked, when someone new was hired, the ritual was to bring in cookies. An email introducing the new addition to the team would go out to about 130 people, and the cookies would be placed at their desk. Now everyone had a reason to swing by and introduce themselves—cookies! It made the new people feel special and welcomed, and was more likely to ease the feeling of anxiety that naturally comes with being the new person.

If you get hired at a cool tech company, you will likely be showered with swag: t-shirts, stickers, and other merch to make you feel like you're part of the team. At Zappos, new hires are given The Culture Book, which is packed with photos of company outings and community service projects from the previous year. The original idea hatched fifteen years ago with a simple goal: Capture what the Zappos culture meant to individual employees, in their own words. At the time, company leaders decided it was worth taking the risk of publishing employees' unedited thoughts about the culture. And they were right.

What can you do to bring a fresh approach to welcoming new hires at your organization? Again, the goal should be helping them love their job. We will assume there are others who will take care of which Slack channels and email distribution lists the person needs to be included in.

At Microsoft, new hires are assigned a buddy.[72] Just like you had on grade-school field trips. A pilot program with 600 employees at the company found onboarding buddies played a pivotal role in a successful start for new hires, especially in three key areas:

- **Providing context.** Because the employee handbook doesn't include the cultural norms, team dynamics, and other subtleties that tenured employees barely notice.

- **Quicker to productivity.** Because having a buddy can dramatically improve how quickly a new hire learns the ropes and can start doing the work.

- **Improve new employee satisfaction.** The pilot program found that new hires with buddies were 23 percent more satisfied with their overall onboarding experience after their first week on the job than those without buddies.

It's not just the new hire who benefits from this system. Being a buddy is mutually beneficial, helping the tenured employee develop communication and support skills.

If you're the new person and your company doesn't have a buddy system, create your own. Pick someone who appears to be especially engaged in the work (and is someone you generally like talking to), and ask that person to be your buddy, mentor, onboarding partner, or whatever term feels comfortable to you.

"The fact is that if you want to excel in a new job, you can't rely on your company's onboarding process to prepare you," says Susan Peppercorn, author of *Ditch Your Inner Critic at Work: Evidence-Based Strategies to Thrive in Your Career.*[73] "You need to take control of your integration."

MAKING IT HAPPEN

- **Take the initiative.** Learn about the onboarding program at your organization. Find a couple people who were recently hired and ask them what they liked and disliked about the onboarding process. Take that feedback to HR or whoever can help you adapt the official program.

- **Make a checklist.** Find two to three people you like working with and ask them to help you build a checklist of things a new hire would want and need to know. Do a search for existing templates to help you get started (there are many online). Offer it to managers who can make it happen—if that's not you.

- **Be a buddy.** Workplace culture can really be impacted one person at a time. Find someone new who would benefit from your knowledge and experience and offer it.

The way you help someone start a new job goes a long way in ensuring that person finds their work fulfilling and engaging. Considering all the hours we spend at work, that's important, even if the job itself isn't one that brings joy on its own.

* * *

In 2018, Bill's company was honored by the *Puget Sound Business Journal* as one of the twenty-five fastest-growing companies in the region. And Bill is the first to admit that he's making the best of what he has, saying with a laugh: "I'd love to be a professional baseball player, but I don't have the skills to do that."

The point here is that even if we don't have our dream job, we can love our work, no matter what industry we happen to end up in. It takes effort and intention, of course, but is within our reach. What Bill has found over the years is a way to build relationships with people, from contractors to customers to his employees. He prioritizes the value and meaning in the work by focusing on the people, instead of the actual work or service his company provides. He's leveraging The Butterfly Impact to the benefit of others, which ends up benefiting him.

"I've enjoyed the fruits and rewards and what it has provided my family. But I couldn't care less about carpet or how it's made or any of that," Bill told me. "I get joy out of helping people work together and come together to help out in the community. Very few people get to do what they truly love. If the rewards are there, I can do the work."

As we will explore in the coming chapters, relationships, and the interactions we have with people at work, are critical components to finding meaning and fulfillment throughout life. As we develop more positive connections with others, The Butterfly Impact will ripple throughout our world. And the world of those around us.

CHAPTER 11

INCLUDE EVERYONE

The more we understand our own privilege, the more aware we will be on how to use it for good.

—RUCHIKA TULSHYAN

DeJuan Hoggard is a reporter and anchor at ABC11 in Raleigh-Durham, North Carolina. He's been a TV journalist for more than a decade, and has experienced his share of challenging assignments. One in particular stands out. In 2018, DeJuan and a photographer traveled to Charlottesville, Virginia, to cover the one-year anniversary of the Unite the Right rally, which had erupted into violent protests. Self-identified white supremacist James Alex Fields, Jr., deliberately plowed his car into a crowd of counter-protesters, killing a woman named Heather Heyer and injuring nineteen other people. (Fields was convicted of first-degree murder plus additional counts, and sentenced to life in prison with an additional 419 years.)

The original Unite the Right rally occurred amidst controversy generated by the removal of Confederate monuments by local governments, following the 2015 mass shooting at a church in Charleston, South Carolina. In the 2015 incident, a white supremacist shot and killed nine Black churchgoers, including the minister Clementa Pinckney, a state senator.

The anniversary rally in 2018 drew only twenty to thirty Unite the Right protesters, while thousands of counter-protesters from religious organizations, civil rights groups, and anti-fascist organizers marched through town. At one point, counter-protesters surrounded DeJuan and photographer Gary Cooper. One person even cut the audio cable on Cooper's camera, a moment that DeJuan posted to Twitter, generating several hundred thousand views and more than a thousand comments.

DeJuan Hoggard ✔
@DeJuanABC11   ···

This is the moment protestors and members of Antifa tried to stop us from filming and then cut our audio cable.

687.4K views   0:00 / 0:21 🔊 ⤢

4:47 PM · Aug 12, 2018 from Charlottesville, VA · Twitter for iPhone

"At no point did we feel scared," DeJuan told me.[74] "Conservatives went nuts with it. Sean Hannity, Tucker Carlson, everyone on Fox News was playing it up and fanning the flames."

As divisive as the country was in 2018, it's hard to imagine a time more divisive than today in the United States. Wearing masks amid the COVID-19 pandemic, opening local businesses, going back to school, playing sports, getting vaccinated—everything seems to have a divisive argument connected to it.

"People just spend so much time in their echo chambers," says DeJuan. Like many other Black journalists, he spent weeks covering Black Lives Matter protests in 2020 as part of his job, trying to balance a personal desire for social change with the professional obligation to cover the story impartially.

DeJuan Hoggard

"When I put my journalist hat on, I can be extremely objective and leave my opinions at the door," DeJuan says. "But I can't leave my blackness at the door."

While covering the wide array of challenges presented in this book, I can't imagine how difficult it would be to tackle them while also having to deal with the discrimination faced by women, people of color, LGBTQ people, people with disabilities, or holders of nontraditional religious beliefs. As an able-bodied, middle class, white, cis-gender male, I have plenty of privilege. Unconscious and implicit bias are real and affect everyone, even people like me who think they have lived their lives on the opposite side of racism, sexism, and other intolerance.

Regardless of how woke any one of us feels about these matters, we live in a system with structures, foundations, and cultural norms that are so well established that they are often difficult to see. Isabel Wilkerson, author of *Caste: The Origins of Our Discontents*, illuminated in her 2020 book the many ways we are unwittingly influenced by factors beyond our control.[75]

"A caste system is an artificial construction, a fixed and embedded ranking of human value that sets the presumed supremacy of one group against the presumed inferiority of other groups," she wrote.

In this chapter and throughout this book, I am going to presume that you want to be more inclusive and less biased, and to thrive in a healthy culture where everyone feels welcomed and accepted. It's just that most people need some help with how to do that. I know I do.

I grew up in northern Idaho—not exactly a hotbed of diversity and inclusion—at a time when an Aryan Nations group was making national headlines for organizing downtown parades and some minor acts of violence. One day, driving home from high school, I turned the corner to see a group of fire trucks in front of the house of Bill Wassmuth, the priest from my church. The group had pipe-bombed his house. Thankfully, no one was injured. Father Bill had become a powerful voice for equality and routinely spoke out against the Aryans, which made him a target.

My hometown eventually rooted out the organized evil of the Aryan Nations, but not before damage had been done. A teenage boy named Rodney and his single mom lived on our street for less than a year. It took immense courage to be two of the very few Black people in a town that had such openly racist factions (plus others in the shadows). The first time I saw Rodney shooting a basketball in his driveway, I walked over to join him; at that time in my life, all I wanted to do was play basketball. I invited him to hang out with my friends on multiple occasions, and he helped us see the world through his eyes, if only a little. He had a quick, biting humor and tried to keep things light, saying things like, "I'm not sitting in back this time. I'm Black. I always have to sit in back." We laughed, nervously at first, but over time we got to know Rodney as a kid who simply wanted to be a teenager, just like the rest of us.

Eventually, Rodney and his mom moved away after someone wrote the N-word on a brick and tossed it through their front window.

These experiences helped shape me and my educational focus for years to come. In high school, I chose Martin Luther King, Jr., as the topic for my high school essay class, where we spent an entire semester writing one paper to prepare for college. Later, in graduate school at the University of North Carolina, I spent more than a year on my thesis project, which detailed the integration of college athletics in the South during the civil rights movement. The final project topped 200 pages and, thanks to a grant from the Park Foundation, I traveled to four states to do primary research at different university libraries and interview key figures from that powerful time in history. My interviewees included Dean Smith, the legendary basketball coach at UNC and one of my all-time favorites, and Charlie Scott, the Black player that Smith recruited in 1966 to break the Atlantic Coast Conference's color barrier.

Integration and equality have been topics of passion for me for as long as I can remember. But like many other white people, I had to reassess my own actions and behaviors in 2020. The senseless killing of George Floyd, Breonna Taylor, Jacob Blake, and others sparked worldwide protests and a new reckoning by companies, organizations, and individuals to make new commitments to diversity and inclusion.

This came on the heels of the #MeToo movement, which had increased awareness of systemic sexual harassment—another reckoning for people like me with the many challenges women face in the workplace simply for being female. Added to this mix is the Pride movement and awareness of the obstacles encountered by LGBTQ people, among which included legalized employment discrimination, until it was successfully overturned by the Supreme Court in 2020. We still have a long way to go before the LGBTQ community can feel fully included socially and culturally, but at least they now have the law on their side.

 **BUTTERFLY IMPACT SIGNPOST**

While one chapter is not nearly enough attention to give these important issues, let's create a foundation, identifying some simple steps to build upon as you work to further the inclusion of those unlike you in your work life. The Butterfly Impact of awareness, appreciation, empathy, and action to counter decades of sexism, racism, and mistreatment of LGBTQ individuals in the workplace will create a ripple effect through your team, your organization, and your personal life, as well.

"The key to moving forward is what we do with our discomfort," says Robin DiAngelo, author of *White Fragility*,[76] a book that shot to the top of bestseller lists in 2020 during the height of the Black Lives Matter movement. While the attention largely focused on racism, and specifically racism toward Black people, the lessons of inclusion that received the spotlight in most organizations also apply to other marginalized groups and individuals who have been treated differently because of their gender, sexuality, ethnicity, religion, or appearance.

As the father of a transgender teen who often prefers to present as gender non-conforming, with brightly dyed hair, loud-colored clothing, and eye-catching footwear, I have seen the stares. The judgment. The derision. When we walk through a restaurant or other public spaces, heads turn. I can almost hear people thinking, *What a freak!* He attended an art school where many, if not most, of his classmates dress similarly, although each one uniquely. In that realm, he is normal. In any other setting, he is viewed as anything but.

How do we address someone who is so different from us? Take this question and apply it to any marginalized group. The goal is not to treat everyone the same. The goal is to understand what systems and structures and cultural norms exist (or have existed) that obstruct, demean, or belittle people who are different. In many cases, people in these groups have been treated as lesser than those with white (and cis-gender male) privilege.

"I haven't really experienced discrimination, it's more ignorance," DeJuan says. "It's not that it doesn't exist, but sometimes people you feel like you know pretty well will say something that is tone deaf, or just not right."

If you are a member of a marginalized group, work as a sales rep, real estate agent, or in some other job that requires you to leave the office and interact with people who are not co-workers, it can be extra challenging. In addition to dealing with unconscious bias or other forms of discrimination in the office, you also may have to face potentially difficult situations with people who are barely more than strangers to you. For journalists like DeJuan, it's a daily challenge, compounded by the complicated and supercharged political environment and unprecedented news cycle of recent years.

"I try to see them with a lens of grace," DeJuan says when he faces discrimination on assignment. "They don't know me. They had that feeling before they even met me. It doesn't excuse any action they take toward me, but I didn't do anything personally toward them. I give them a little space to air their grievance until it gets to the point where I fear my safety."

Fortunately, DeJuan doesn't scare easily. "I've been in plenty of places…but the only things I'm scared of is my mom and spiders."

Once we have empathy and uncover our unconscious biases, we can address that privilege and our place in these structures. Only then can we help one another see where racism, sexism, and other discrimination is happening in our organizations.

"White people raised in Western society are conditioned into a white supremacist worldview because it is the bedrock of our society and its institutions," DiAngelo writes in *White Fragility*. "Regardless of whether a parent told you that everyone was equal, or the poster in the hall of your white suburban school proclaimed the value of diversity, or you have traveled abroad, or you have people of color in your workplace or family, the ubiquitous socializing power of white supremacy cannot be avoided."

Have you ever been asked to smile more at work? I have not. It happens all the time to women, who are also subjected to mansplaining and forced to manage advances from men with higher authority.

"Everyday sexism and racism—also known as microaggressions—can take many forms," according to the annual Women in the Workplace report from LeanIn.org and McKinsey & Co. "Microaggressions are forms of everyday discrimination, like sexism or racism. They signal disrespect and reflect inequality."[77]

The 2019 report found that 73 percent of women report experiencing everyday microaggressions or discrimination. These are both rooted in bias—the same bias that impacts other, even more marginalized groups. It also impacts how much women and other minorities earn for the same work. In 2020, women made only 81 cents for every dollar a man made, according to the annual Payscale Salary Survey.[78] Black men earn 87 cents for every dollar a white man earns. Hispanic or Latino men have the next largest gap as they earn 91 cents for every dollar earned by a white man.

The same Payscale Survey study in 2020 found that, by calculating presumptive raises given over a forty-year career, women in an uncontrolled group stand to lose $900,000 on average over a lifetime.

The challenges of creating a truly inclusive workplace are daunting, but obviously important—even for a minority corporate founder, like Rafat Ali, one of the more successful media entrepreneurs of my generation. I first met Rafat years ago, when I invited him to participate in a two-day workshop that I was helping to lead in Florida for journalists looking to start their own business, as he had successfully done.

Rafat has started two companies over the past fifteen years that combined employed a couple hundred people. As an immigrant himself representing the perspective of a Muslim and an ethnic minority, Rafat has been outspoken online about all forms of injustice, openly acknowledging his own reckoning on how much more he and his company need to do.

"Like many companies, we should constantly be aware of unconscious bias and structural racism at our organization and in our industry," says Rafat, most recently the CEO and founder of Skift, an online news and information company serving the travel industry.[79]

How do we go beyond "diversity training" and boilerplate messaging on corporate websites to make substantial changes in this realm? Ruchika Tulshyan is working on a new book that will focus on inclusion in the workplace and the actions people can take—from tackling unconscious bias to listening actively—and all the stories she is including in the book are from women of color. Ruchika, whose previous book is *The Diversity Advantage: Fixing Gender Inequality in the Workplace*, is an adjunct professor at Seattle University whose classes I've spoken to over the years. She hadn't settled on a name for her new book when I spoke to her, but she said she was leaning toward "Inclusion on Purpose" or something similar.

Ruchika Tulshyan

"The more we understand our own privilege, the more aware we will be of how to use it for good," says Ruchika, who grew up in Singapore and has spent her professional career in the US as a minority woman of color.[80]

"If you're male and White, for example, (and) you see a fellow co-worker showing behaviors of discrimination, you don't have much to lose. It's your responsibility to speak up."

Even though her book won't be published until 2022, Ruchika was kind enough to offer some concrete suggestions based on her research to help bring this chapter to a close.

"IF YOU'RE MALE AND WHITE, FOR EXAMPLE, (AND) YOU SEE A FELLOW CO-WORKER SHOWING BEHAVIORS OF DISCRIMINATION, YOU DON'T HAVE MUCH TO LOSE. IT'S YOUR RESPONSIBILITY TO SPEAK UP."

MAKING IT HAPPEN

The main point Ruchika has been trying to make with her work is that truly understanding diversity and inclusion is a lifelong journey and cannot be achieved by taking a training class, attending a panel discussion, or even participating in an all-day workshop. The field keeps evolving, and new awareness is constantly emerging. Here are her recommendations:

- **Name it.** Name issues like racism or sexism exactly for what they are. Previously we had to find different ways to name these issues, and people used a lot of euphemisms. Today it's important to cut straight to the chase. Race really does impact a person's trajectory. Women really do face a different work environment. Call it out for what it is.

- **Inquire.** If someone makes an insensitive comment or is making decisions with unconscious bias, take the person aside and ask, "Can you tell me what you were thinking?" Ruchika emphasized the importance of assuming positive intent with the person, instead of going on the attack. Her suggested language includes: "You're a really good person.

Here's how I heard this. I'm confident that is not what you meant; can you give me clarification?"

- **Invest.** It doesn't have to feel adversarial. Feedback feels negative if you don't show you're invested in that person's success and growth.

- **Be active.** The most important action step everyone can take is to stand up to bias. "You can be a passive ally all you want, but we need passive allies to become active advocates," she told me.

Ruchika's recommendations align with lessons we will learn in the coming chapters about listening and engaging with people. It turns out that listening to other human beings—really listening to them—can help solve many of the challenges we face in dealing with one another.

We can't be perfect, but we can make progress.

I asked DeJuan if he saw big changes in 2020 when the Black Lives Matter protest movement exploded and became part of the daily conversation, at work and everywhere else.

"From a messaging standpoint, yes," DeJuan said. "There's not nearly as much pushback or opposition to stories that we want to do for our Black community. Are people doing it because they are checking off a box, or as something that needs to be done? Maybe. But we're moving in the right direction."

CHAPTER 12

WORK IS SOCIAL. WHICH MEANS OTHER PEOPLE.

You are the product of the people you spend the most time with.
—LIZ PEARCE

Brad Thompson says it looked like a "dream job," at least on paper. Working in corporate sales in the newly emerging field of cellular communication in the 1990s, Brad had courtside tickets to entertain clients at NBA games. He took clients to NFL and Major League Baseball games, too, in addition to lavish dinners and golf outings, all in pursuit of signing the next deal. Brad also enjoyed lunches, drinks, and dinners with his colleagues.

Sounds like a recipe for workplace happiness, right?

However, the company had divided Brad's sales team into vertical markets, which left some ambiguity about whom each rep could sell to. That meant there were often conflicts within the sales team around who should get to capture which business, and that created a sticky situation for Brad.

"One of the reasons I had to get out of that business was I had people that I would have lunch with, or go have drinks with, and [they] would look at me and act like they were my best work friend. And at the same time, they were stealing business from me," Brad told me.[81] "That was my income. This is not at all what I thought a team was all about. I don't know who could define a team in those terms."

Brad says the situation didn't meet his own personal code of ethics. It felt unfulfilling to have hollow relationships. But he felt he had to find a way to make it work—he had a new marriage, a new mortgage, and two young sons. Trying to conform to the realities of that world led him to a psychological place he didn't anticipate.

"I was starting to take advantage of other people. I was starting to figure out the system and survive and meet my goals," says Brad, who has been one of my closest friends since college. "Because at the end of the month it didn't matter. All it is, is performance-based. They don't care how you get there.

"For some personalities that's fine; they thrive on that. That's not my personality; that's not where my strengths come from."

Not all sales jobs are so cutthroat, of course. But Brad's experience drove him to search for other career options, particularly something that would make him feel like part of a true team. He became interested in working as a firefighter after a lifelong friend joined the fire department.

He studied hard, trained hard, and eventually received an opportunity to switch careers from corporate sales to firefighter. He jumped at the chance. At first, it did not go well.

"I really struggled the first six months to put all the skills together, and I had two young kids at home—one was under one—and I thought I wasn't going to make it," Brad told me. "When I started, although I had been working out hard, working in the gym doesn't equate. It [firefighting] was a very mechanical mindset, and I didn't have a lot of experience in that. I didn't think I would make it through probation, because there were certain tasks that I was just struggling with, and that was pretty stressful."

You know what else was pretty stressful? Making about one-third as much money as a firefighter as he did in his corporate sales job. Brad had gone from a six-figure salary, entertaining clients with courtside seats, to practicing how to tie ropes and throw ladders in order to save his job.

"It got to the point where either I had to step up or they were going to start the process of trying to get rid of me," Brad says.

A young firefighter on Brad's shift brought him into the training room with the rest of the firefighters on that crew, and told him they were not going to let him fail. They told him he was struggling just because he lacked confidence.

"They said 'We have your back. We will do whatever you possibly need to get you through this. We will drill with you any time of the day. We are here for twenty-four hours, so if we need to train in the middle of the night, let's do it'" is the message Brad remembers hearing that day.

Brad Thompson

Over the next several months, they worked with him constantly. Brad felt he needed to show them that he was doing everything he could to work really hard. His teammates would come out and help, even though there would be no personal benefit to any of them, whether Brad made it through probation or not.

"It's the complete opposite of sales," Brad says, pointing to his previous experience. "They were rallying around the guy that was struggling. I had never really experienced that kind of support."

More than twenty years later, Brad is still with the fire department. He continued to work hard to learn everything he could and improve in his job and received one promotion after another. In 2021 he was promoted to fire chief of the Valley Regional Fire Authority, overseeing operations for the entire department of 120 people. Needless to say, he does not regret that career change back in the '90s.

As we saw in Part 1, the vast majority of employees in the US do not feel engaged at work. Framing it as a job or task problem, however, misses the full picture. Let's add another element to what makes for a meaningful, engaging work experience: *what* you do, *why* you do it, and *whom* you do it with.

"All the studies show that your relationships make the most impact on your happiness in the long run," says Liz Pearce. "You are the product of the people you spend the most time with."

 BUTTERFLY IMPACT SIGNPOST

We need to recognize and appreciate the impact other people have on our workplace well-being. You can't control anyone else's behavior towards you, but you can change the way you behave, with an eye toward strengthening relationships at work. The Butterfly Impact means it will also help strengthen the relationships you have with family, friends, and everyone else in your life. The ripple effect of kindness and happiness and treating others well will contribute to a positive culture in all facets of your life.

You don't have to be a manager or supervisor to offer positive feedback to colleagues. Even those above you on the organizational chart. It's well known that if you want to influence a certain behavior in other people, offer praise for the behavior you want (instead of complaining about the behavior you don't want).

It can be as simple as being more of a "giver" and less of a "taker," according to Adam Grant. He's the author of *Give and Take: A*

Revolutionary Approach to Success. In his book, Grant found that "givers"[82]—the supportive people who enjoy sharing their expertise and helping the careers of others—enjoy more career success, in addition to being generally happier.

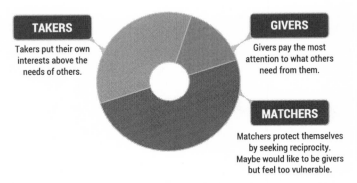

TAKERS

Takers put their own interests above the needs of others.

GIVERS

Givers pay the most attention to what others need from them.

MATCHERS

Matchers protect themselves by seeking reciprocity. Maybe would like to be givers but feel too vulnerable.

Givers, Takers, and Matchers graphic reenvisioned with permission from Adam Grant.

It's true, giving makes us happy. Research by University of British Columbia professor Elizabeth Dunn found that when subjects are given $5 with instructions to give the money to a stranger, their happiness increases more than that of subjects who are given $20 to spend on themselves.[83] I'm not recommending you walk around the office handing out five-dollar bills to your co-workers (although it might be a fun experiment), but think about what you can offer.

It might be as simple as just listening that makes the difference.

THE POWER OF LISTENING

"One of the biggest gifts we can give anyone is the gift of being heard," says William Ury,[84] co-founder of Harvard's Program on Negotiation and one of the world's best-known and most influential experts on negotiation. "With the simple power of listening now, we can transform our relationships, our families, and our world for the better."

Listening is simple, but not always easy. When I am listening to someone, and my brain is about to vomit one of my great ideas back at the person, I try really hard to stop. Then I ask a follow-up question, inviting the speaker to go deeper, to share more, to explain again. I don't get it right every time, but I know this is what true listening looks like. And like so many other facets of life, I get a little better at it each time I try.

Bob Chapman, who, in the Introduction to this book, acquainted us with the radical idea that caring for people is good for business, couldn't agree more. "The single most important thing we have learned in our company is we need to teach people to listen to each other, which is the key to caring."[85]

Chapman's company offers training on listening, and employees flock to the course. The stated goal of the course is to improve leadership, but the feedback is usually not work-related.

"When we teach how to listen at work to be better leaders, they don't tell us they ran a better accounting department or sales department," Chapman says. "They say to us my marriage has never been better and my teenage daughters are talking to me."

One of the keys to becoming a better listener is learning to listen to ourselves first, according to Ury.

"What makes it so hard to listen is that there's so much going on in our minds, so much noise and distraction that we don't have the mental and emotional space to listen to the other side," says Ury, coauthor of *Getting to Yes*, the best-selling negotiation book of all time. He recommends taking a few moments first to quiet your mind and then just tune in—to listen to where you are. "I believe that if we did that, we would find it a lot easier to listen to others."

This concept is powerful because it reduces the pressure on us to have something perfect to say in recognition of a colleague or teammate. The power in an interaction that starts with "What are you working on?" and ends with "That is so cool, nicely done!" has a ripple effect across the team, the organization, and your little corner of the world. As a giver, you offered the other person an opportunity to share their unique gifts, and in doing so you increased your own happiness and well-being by investing in others. Through listening, you can create a brief social connection that has many positive health and happiness consequences for both parties.

"I always thought when you care for someone, you go over and talk to them," Chapman says. "It turns out when you care for someone, you go over to listen to them with empathy, which is a teachable skill. When we teach that in our business, it profoundly changes people's relationships when they feel valued."

The Butterfly Impact of listening is powerful, too. According to Ury, "Listening can be a chain reaction, in which each person who feels genuinely listened to can be inspired to listen to the next. Listening can be contagious."

Do you know what else is contagious? Enthusiasm. Energy. Vibes. One of the secrets to a happy work life is being around people with positive energy who make you feel engaged. If you feel listened to, and really heard, you want to share that feeling, too.

"There's no magic bullet, but there are things that I do as sort of a practice to set myself up for enjoying work, and a lot of it is about people," says Elaine Helm, a public relations executive and the person who introduced me to Mark Mohammadpour (Chapter 3).[86] "I like seeking out the people in the organization that I want to spend time with so that, day-to-day, I'm surrounded by the type of energy that I want, not the negative energy."

Psychologists call this emotional contagion, which can be loosely defined as the unconscious transmission of actions or emotions from one individual to another. In her 2002 study "The Ripple Effect: Emotional Contagion and Its Influence on Group Behavior," Sigal G. Barsade called human beings "walking mood inductors."[87] We are continuously influencing the feelings, judgments, and behaviors of others.

"I've learned that people will forget what you said, people will forget what you did, but people will never forget how you made them feel," Maya Angelou famously observed.

Seeking out positive energy takes effort, of course, and knowing the difference between what you can control and what you can't control. How you show up, and what emotional contagion you spread, are both powerful and under your control—at work, at home, and in life.

"Being enthusiastic is worth twenty-five IQ points," according to Kevin Kelly, Senior Maverick for *Wired*, a magazine he helped co-found twenty-five years ago.[88] "It's about people who are obsessively interested. They are making things happen and they have a deep interest that I think is often the fountain and the foundation of big new things."

Think about the people in your life, especially those at work. Whom would you describe as enthusiastic? Are those people the ones you enjoy working with the most? The answer is most likely yes. Now the challenge is, how do you show up with more enthusiasm so you can be one of those people? (If you aren't already, of course.)

Enthusiasm is difficult to measure, especially in the workplace. It's often subjective, and introverted people may feel that it's an advantage extroverts possess. What I appreciate about how Kelly defines enthusiasm is that it's being "obsessively interested," not jumping up and down, or being loud, like a high school cheerleader. We can increase how interested we are in the current project or meeting, or the person we are meeting with. It just takes a little more effort and some additional focus.

"I'm often not the smartest person in the room, but I'm very often the most enthusiastic person in the room, and I will get invited back," Kelly says.

"All emotions—joy, fear, sadness, and stress—have been shown to be contagious," says Elaine Hatfield, who co-authored the book *Emotional Contagion* way back in 1983.[89] The Butterfly Impact of your positive emotional contagion can be a powerful force in your happiness, increasing your engagement and fulfillment at work and helping you be a better partner, spouse, parent, friend, or teammate outside of work.

As Brad Thompson discovered, the people around you at work can build you up or tear you down. If you feel energized—and challenged—by people you appreciate and respect at work, you will have a much better chance at thriving in your job. Before pointing the finger at others, though, take a moment to consider how you are showing up for the people at your job and in your life.

MAKING IT HAPPEN

People are complex creatures. They often have outsized influence on our happiness and well-being, but we can take more control over how we influence other people in a positive way. Here's how to get started:

- **Stop.** Take a moment before you initiate conversation, and listen to yourself. What's going on in your head? Make some space up there before you try to engage someone else.

- **Recognize.** Set a goal of offering praise or recognition to someone at work once a week. Gradually increase the goal until it's at least once a day.

- **Listen.** Practice genuine listening with your colleagues at work. Ask someone about their current work, or a challenge they are facing. Then ask for more information.

- **Bring enthusiasm.** Pick something every day that you can be "obsessively interested" in. Share that interest with those around you. Spread positive emotional contagion. And seek out those who do the same.

We should all want to live in a world with more recognition, listening, and enthusiasm. These simple recommendations are not easy to turn into habits, however. Why? Because we often feel too busy to make time for them. Don't let that hold you back. Prioritize these activities and track them. You will be amazed to see how big an impact this makes on you personally.

Thinking about what Brad went through when he transitioned from corporate sales to firefighter, the life-changing difference we can all make lies in how we support other people. Helping others at work really does help us help ourselves.

CHAPTER 13

MAKE RELATIONSHIPS MATTER AT WORK

You can't just sit back and wait for someone else. You have to go get it. Or create it yourself.

—NICOLE THOMAS

Nicole Thomas is smart, driven, and tireless. She earned an undergraduate degree in marketing and two master's degrees in the span of five years, then set off on a career to help organizations and their corporate social responsibility efforts.

While working for a *Fortune* 100 company, she seized an opportunity to lead a pilot project that would be huge for her budding career. She didn't have a budget or resources, and gave up her planned two-week vacation to lead the company's first foray into NASCAR sponsorship. She also didn't have much of a team, and had to forge relationships with other groups to make this project happen. She learned valuable lessons that would shape the path of her career.

"Here I was, as a Black woman, being able to design a race car," Nicole told me.[90] "I saw it as an opportunity to create a high-profile project by myself. Everyone who worked with me said I was easy to work with."

Nicole Thomas

While her project was hailed internally, she didn't get to celebrate that success. When it came time for the race, Nicole was told there were no additional tickets for her to attend. Later she learned that one of the higher-ups took his twelve-year-old son.

You can only be 50 percent of any relationship, which is something I learned going through hours of counseling trying to save two marriages. The other half is in someone else's hands, or if you are at work, several others' hands. In Nicole's situation, she had done her part for the company, but the people around her missed the opportunity to reciprocate.

"The next (year) they gave the project to a white woman who got resources, tickets to the event, a big dinner," Nicole says. "I was able to see these disparities, and I realized I have to own my career."

Nicole is now thriving as the founder of her own marketing and communications agency, helping clients such as Phillip Rix, the go-to chocolatier for Stevie Wonder, and other celebrities. She's also helping organizations develop and manage their diversity and inclusion efforts. Relationships are fundamental to her business model, and Nicole has proven that she is someone other people can rely on. Her career story—like Brad Thompson's in the last chapter—has two acts: the first act, without the right relationships at work, and the second act, in which our protagonist finds the right people to provide the other 50 percent of the relationship.

"You have to realize it's up to you," Nicole told me, referring to how important it is to feel like a valued member of a team. "Removing that sense of helplessness...I wasn't putting something that important in someone else's hands any longer. You can't just sit back and wait for someone else. You have to go get it. Or create it yourself."

As we learned in the last chapter, whom you work with can make or break your experience. Nicole has no regrets about moving on from her previous role. The people around her were making decisions that were frustrating and felt unfair to her. Have you had a similar experience? Or ever lost sleep over some knucklehead at work? It's maddening.

I once worked with someone who had an extreme Jekyll-and-Hyde personality, and was constantly creating drama in the organization or cutting someone down in a meeting. On a Mr. Hyde day, this person could say something that would burrow into my emotional soft tissue. I wouldn't flinch at work; instead, I would hide behind my professional shield, the one that allowed me to dismiss the incident as nothing but bluster. Yet I would lie awake at night, replaying the scene from earlier in the day in my head, and eventually grow more and more upset with myself that I was letting this person ruin my sleep.

"You can have a great job, with purpose, with a good salary and free food, but nothing will compensate for a poisonous relationship in the workplace," says Esther Perel, a relationship psychologist, author, and podcast host who was named to Oprah Winfrey's Supersoul 100 list of visionaries and influential leaders.[91] "You go to bed every night fretting about someone who is sleeping perfectly fine. And that eats people up."

I have witnessed more dysfunctional work relationships than I care to count. Watching smart, ambitious, and otherwise wonderful people lock horns in a meeting, or undermine one another with passive-aggressive comments in the hallway, is one of the more challenging and exasperating parts of my job as a consultant. It's often the area where I feel like I can make the biggest impact, too, since relationships at work are generally not given the attention they deserve. We hire people, give them titles, set up meetings, and establish goals, then expect everyone to mesh like a symphony when, all too often, the collective sound is a cacophony. *Just think of your days in band class in junior high.*

"The most fundamental, powerful, and enduring fuel for performance is a feeling of safety and trust—in ourselves and in the world around us," according to *New York Times* columnist Tony Schwartz.[92] "Most of us spend the greatest percentage of our waking lives in the workplace. But how much energy and capacity do we squander each day worrying about being criticized by our bosses, in conflict and competition with colleagues, or fielding complaints from clients and customers?"

In addition to making or breaking productivity and performance at work, interpersonal dynamics are core to our overall well-being. Perel, channeling none other than Sigmund Freud, compared relationships in work and love: "In both, we experience a sense of identity, a sense of belonging, a sense of continuity, and hopefully, a sense of self-worth and fulfillment."

This is the power of The Butterfly Impact, since our happiness and well-being are based upon relationships in all facets of our lives. "If you are not satisfied at work, you take that frustration home, lie awake thinking about work, affecting your loved ones," Perel added.

 **BUTTERFLY IMPACT SIGNPOST**

Thankfully, the opposite scenario is also true: Strong social connections at work make people happier and physically healthier, less stressed, more engaged, and more productive. Dynamic, fun relationships at work are also a well-lit path to really enjoying your job. The people you work with are often the difference between a job you love and one you loathe. Just think about how much time you spend with co-workers, compared to time with family and friends. *Or maybe that's too depressing.*

"Not everyone's gonna like you," says Liz Pearce.[93] Before we dive into the tactics and strategies around building better relationships at work, I think it's important to level-set our perspective on the issue, and I love what Liz offers on the subject:

"Some people are going to actively undermine you. They really don't matter. We're all just the main characters in our own story. Something that is happening to you will paint you in a bad light. Most people are not thinking about you, they are thinking about themselves. What happens to you is of very little consequence. No one cares as much about me as I do."

This is the lesson that Nicole Thomas used as motivation to create her own path—one that gives her control over whom she works with and the relationships she forges in her job. If you are among the majority of people who don't get to choose *whom* you work with, the question is, *how* do you develop stronger relationships at work? How do you form bonds where there is friction? *And can't we all just get along?*

A TEAM YOU CAN TRUST

"Remember teamwork begins by building trust," says Patrick Lencioni, author of *The Five Dysfunctions of a Team: A Leadership Fable*.[94] "Trust is knowing that when a team member does push you, they're doing it because they care about the team."

Good team relationships are good for business, too, according to Lencioni. "Not finance. Not strategy. Not technology. It is teamwork that remains the ultimate competitive advantage, both because it is so powerful and so rare."

Let's take a closer look at fear of conflict and building trust, two of the five dysfunctions identified by Lencioni, as well as what to do when repair is needed in a work relationship. The Butterfly Impact of learning to improve your work relationships is how much better you will be with the other relationships in your life, too. As you read, think of how these concepts might apply to your partner, spouse, children, siblings, or friends.

The fear of conflict is human nature. It drives us to present ourselves at work as always knowing the answer, to always having the right idea. Remember our aversion to temporary incompetence from Chapter 3? People want to be seen as smart and capable at work—and there's nothing wrong with that.

Unfortunately, no one is always right, not even the boss. Often there is a need for a team to choose between more than one good idea. Hello, conflict! Teams that haven't built trust are particularly predisposed to find themselves at odds with one another. The worst part of this real-world scenario is that these conflicts accumulate over time, making it even more difficult for true teamwork to form.

What can you do to combat this situation? Become a "miner of conflict," which Lencioni describes as someone who unearths buried disagreements within the team and sheds the light of day on them. It takes courage and confidence to call out sensitive issues and force team members to work through them. Learn to ask questions, so that everyone feels genuinely listened to. Try to emotionally detach from the issue on the table as you do this. It's more important to help a team or small group work through conflict than it is to have your idea win the day.

Consultants are encouraged to "read the room," which means to pay close attention to the nonverbal cues of the people around the table. Most people are not professional poker players, and do a fairly poor job of hiding how they feel about the current conversation—something I learned soon after starting my job as a consultant. You just have to notice. While this is an essential job function for consultants, everyone can benefit from the practice.

If a colleague or teammate is visibly frustrated by a decision, or shuts down in a meeting after his or her idea is passed over, stop the meeting and go back. "You seem to have a lot of energy around this" is one way to approach someone whose voice is getting louder (and has started waving their arms and pounding on the table). "Is there more that we should know?" Or, in the case of someone who is shut down, try something as simple as, "I want to make sure you were able to fully explain your idea. Is there anything else you would like us to know?" The goal is to build a team dynamic where anyone can ask for more information in a meeting, and to use it as a tool to "mine for conflict" in a non-threatening way. The more often it happens, the more trust will build among the team and leadership.

The more trust, the less conflict. Building trust, however, is not easy. Trust has three core drivers, according to Harvard professor Frances Frei and Anne Morriss, co-authors of *Unleashed: The Unapologetic Leader's Guide to Empowering Everyone Around You:*[95]

- **Authenticity.** I experience the real you.

- **Logic.** I know you can do it; your reasoning and judgment are sound.

- **Empathy.** I believe you care about me and my success.

AUTHENTICITY
I experience the real you.

LOGIC
I know you can do it; your reasoning and judgment are sound.

EMPATHY
I believe you care about me and my success.

How to build a triangle of trust.

People tend to trust you when they believe that they are inter-acting with the real you (authenticity), when they have faith in your judgment and competence (logic), and when they feel that you care about them (empathy). When trust is absent or lost, it can often be traced back to a breakdown in one of these drivers. When you are weak on any one of the three, Frei says, you have a "trust wobble." And everyone has a trust wobble on occasion. *I also have a healthy eating wobble, a saving money wobble and...*

"To identify your (trust) wobble, think of a recent moment when you were not as trusted as you want to be. Maybe someone simply doubted your ability to execute," Frei and Morriss wrote in the *Harvard Business Review*.[96] "With that story in mind, do something hard: Give the other person in your story the benefit of the doubt. Call that person your 'skeptic.' Assume that person's reservations are valid and that you were the one responsible for the breakdown in trust. This exercise only works if you own it."

Trust is a macro-level workplace phenomenon that builds or erodes slowly over time. It takes patience, recognition, and focus to build great trust, especially when it doesn't come naturally with certain co-workers and colleagues. No one gets along perfectly with everyone. There are going to be bumps in the road, moments of disconnect and friction and frustration, just as there are with any relationship.

A few years ago, shortly after I started working with a new corporate team that oversaw a group of local TV stations, I hit one of these bumps—hard. A small group of high-level company officers and I had collaborated to design an ambitious plan of transformation for all of the stations in the group. It was my role to visit the stations and help them implement the plans through a series of meetings and workshops. In a string of emails and a couple conference calls, it was suggested that someone from the corporate team dial into the meetings to ensure alignment between what I was presenting and the direction from the division team. I felt a lack of trust in me—a distrust that I would be faithful to the plan we had all contributed to. It hurt. I didn't like the idea on an emotional level, so I pushed back. It didn't go well.

After a couple heated conversations and email exchanges, I realized that I was having an emotional reaction to feeling a lack of trust. No one likes that feeling. Once I recognized that, I could move forward with repairing the relationship. Instead of digging in on my position, I asked for more information from the other side. This "conflict mining" helped shine a light on the issue and made it easier to work through it. Repair was essential, because I was hoping these relationships would last for years. Thankfully, they have, and continue to get stronger every day.

While trust may be macro, the building and repair of trust are micro: small actions or behaviors that may seem inconsequential in the moment, but add up to define your co-worker relationships. Think of them as "micromoves."

"Micromoves are like the steps that characterize a dance," according to business professors Kerry Roberts Gibson and Beth Schinoff.[97] "You take a step, and then your co-worker takes a step.

"Each step, or micromove, can change the direction of the relationship. A small act of gratitude or compassion—like saying 'thank you' when someone holds a door open, or being understanding when someone is late for a meeting—can bring people together and help build long-term trust."

These small acts are a great way to begin repairing a relationship that has started to wobble. They are easy to do, cost little to nothing, and take relatively little time. The key is recognizing that a relationship requires repair. Once you do that, you can take it to the next level.

MAKING IT HAPPEN

A team of researchers reviewed 300 management and psychology studies focusing on workplace relationships, relationship transgressions, and relationship repair that had been published in the last fifteen years. They identified three practices that can help you repair and strengthen your work relationships, make them more resilient and able to handle conflict and everyday tensions.[98]

- **Reset the emotional tone.** First, raise the issue. Then set a meeting—a couple days out to let your emotions cool off—in which you can commit to a shared relationship goal.

- **Craft a shared narrative.** What went wrong? Listen first, then focus the discussion on your relationship and reflect on your history, highlighting those times when it worked well.

- **Build relational agility.** Instead of "digging in," pause and improvise; look for a different and creative approach to solve the problem.

As you invest more time and energy in your workplace relationships, focus on these three key practices:

- Address conflict with vulnerability and listening.

- Build trust with authenticity, logic, empathy (and micro-moves).

- Repair relationship wobbles with a reset.

When you develop greater awareness of your workplace relationships and your ability to strengthen them, you will also develop skills that can improve your relationships outside of work, as well. This is The Butterfly Impact at its best. Fewer sleepless nights are nice, too.

✶ ✶ ✶

Looking back on that flare-up of mistrust that I experienced, I have to chuckle. I remember going on a weekend backpacking trip around that time and struggling to get my mind away from the dysfunctional episode in that work relationship. There I was, on a trail in the breathtaking Olympic Mountains with one of my best friends, and I couldn't stop thinking about what someone had written in an email a few days before. In keeping with Esther Perel's observations that were noted at the beginning of this chapter, it was eating me up.

While one of the people involved in that situation has since moved on to a different company, the other person is, I can confidently say, the other half of one of the strongest, healthiest, most productive work partnerships I've ever had. When our weekly one-on-one call gets postponed because of a time conflict, I'm actually a little sad. We have learned to lean on one another, especially when we were going through the pandemic, working together to support stressed-out workers on the front lines of a relentless, months-long breaking news cycle. In writing this chapter, I realized just how healthy our work relationship has become over time.

Jennifer Mitchell and I had to work at the relationship. It didn't come automatically. We only see each other in person a few times a year, which made it even more challenging. It's authentic, with empathy and a shared respect for one another, and we have forged a bond that will not be easily broken.

CHAPTER 14

YOU ARE THE CULTURE

"I've learned that leading in whatever role you're in—modeling your behavior or your interactions—builds that culture, piece by piece."

—ELAINE HELM

Have you ever felt you've been given the responsibility to complete a project at work but don't have the authority to really make it happen? Most of us have been there at some point. It's frustrating to clearly see what needs to happen next, while the people you're relying on to actually get it done sit on the sidelines, often because they have too much on their plate.

Sharon Prill ran into this challenge early in her career. A skillful project manager in her twenties, she found herself leading a massive transformation project for a company filled with leaders who were decades her senior. All the stakeholders were VPs with their own teams and territory.

"I had to do so much politicking and work through so many layers," Sharon recalls.[99] "The people who actually were needed to do the work were several layers down, and everyone was speaking different [work] languages.

"The culture didn't allow for that quick empowerment, so I spent most of my time getting people to see eye to eye."

Sharon Prill

Sharon cares deeply about work culture—and getting things done. Quick, decisive action is her hallmark. The first time I met her, she invited me to lunch to discuss how our respective companies could join forces to solve a problem for the websites we were running at the time. About five minutes into our lunch meeting, she asked me if I wanted to come work for her. I nearly spat out my water, then gathered myself and said, "Maybe?" I had not anticipated getting a job offer completely out of nowhere, but the idea of working with Sharon intrigued me. I could already tell that we shared similar values, and her positive energy was infectious. Sitting across the table from me, Sharon had a similar feeling, an intuition, that I would fit with the culture she was trying to build.

"A lot of people don't realize how much of what you accomplish is due to culture," says Sharon, who has held leadership positions in companies large and small, from startups to legacy industry leaders. She has seen many different work cultures, some that have worked and many that have not. The ones that worked best, she says, are the ones where she had the opportunity to build a culture with her own hires, rather than having to try to create a subculture within a bigger company.

"You have to be very deliberate about what you want from the culture," Sharon told me. "If you do not define it, then you're allowing it to just happen."

I did go on to work for her at *The News Tribune*, but within a couple years she moved on to a bigger and better opportunity out of state. She remains one of the most effective and impactful leaders I've had the pleasure to work with, and I'm grateful to still call her a friend—more than fifteen years after I nearly spat water on her at a fancy waterfront restaurant in Seattle.

"Culture eats strategy for breakfast" has always been one of my favorite sayings.[100] Even as I've spent years trying to help teams avoid this eventuality. For many organizations, it's as predictable as boring meetings, too many emails, and overly complex healthcare benefits. Culture can feel like both an immovable object and an irresistible force within many organizations.

You've probably experienced some version of this scenario: A small group of managers and company leaders spend hours in off-site meetings or day-long strategic planning sessions to develop a comprehensive plan that will transform the company. The managers, full of energy and a gratifying sense of accomplishment, return to the office to unveil the new master plan to the rest of the organization—and are greeted with a collective shrug, sigh, eye roll, or worse. The well-crafted and wordsmithed plan is dead on arrival because the people who are tasked with executing it impose their culture on it, something that the managers didn't consider. Strategy is no match for the status quo.

Culture isn't just capable of eating your organization's strategy. It can devour individual engagement, happiness, fulfillment, and joy. A mountain of research on workplace cultures focuses predominantly on the organization, specifically on execution, productivity, and business strategy. While those factors are all important, what about the people who suffer or thrive, depending on the culture where they work?

Tom Davis remembers a point early in his career when people were clearly suffering where he worked. "Someone told someone but no one told everyone," and there was plenty of "B.S. infighting and cliques," according to Davis.[101] We've all worked there at some point in our career, right? I know I have.

Davis needed a new approach. The lack of communication on his team and the disconnect between his team and others in the organization was ruining his workplace well-being.

His simple solution? A new mantra: "No drama, no surprises," says Davis, now vice president of news at 6ABC in Philadelphia, one of the most dominant and successful local TV stations in the US. "Most everything blows up because of a lack of communication."

A crappy culture will surely slow any business down and make it more difficult to achieve goals and hit performance benchmarks. But that's not the real problem. A toxic culture can ruin a person's life. Nine out of ten American workers, about 130 million people, go home every day feeling they work for an organization that doesn't listen to or care about them. Sadly, research also found that the rate of heart attacks goes up 20 percent on Monday morning. As *The New York Times* reported in 2006, several studies found that deaths from heart attacks follow a pattern with a significant jump on Mondays, then a drop on Tuesdays and the rest of the week.[102]

Culture is not some touchy-feely nicety that only Silicon Valley startups can afford to have. It's vital to your health and well-being. And thankfully, you can do something about it.

 **BUTTERFLY IMPACT SIGNPOST**

Using The Butterfly Impact as our lens, we see that a poor workplace culture will inevitably infect each person's life outside of work, too. It only gets worse if your culture is truly toxic or fully dysfunctional. If you think this is management's responsibility, you're partially right. The ability to create and foster a great culture so people will thrive is one of the best traits of great leaders. Waiting for someone else to fix it leads to feeling powerless, however. You can do more than sit back and complain about the culture at your workplace. Again, your health and well-being are at stake.

Here's the secret: You are the culture.

Everything you do at work—every interaction, conversation, email, chat message, smile, laugh, sigh, eye roll, presentation, meeting invitation, and video call—constitutes some part of the culture where you work. Once you understand and accept this reality—and this power—you can help build the culture you want, instead of the culture you have.

Build the culture you want instead of the culture you have.

"'When I was younger, I felt less empowered to influence the culture," says Elaine Helm, the PR executive we met in Chapter 13. "I didn't really try to balance the long hours and stress with some degree of self-care. When you're in the early part of your career, you feel like you have less influence. But I've learned that leading in whatever role you're in—modeling your behavior or your interactions—builds that culture, piece by piece. People notice and start to adopt it and make it part of how they behave.

"There's a lot you can do day to day that will help you feel better about what you're doing, instead of bringing home stress."

Every individual can impact the culture at work, for better or worse. I remember leading a strategy workshop for a client company a couple years ago, followed by a discussion and brainstorming session in the executive conference room with about twenty leaders from the organization. I thought the session went really well, and ended with some specific action steps to move the team forward. Someone I respect said with a chuckle, a bit of a smile, and raised eyebrows, "Too bad that's not how things are done here." Ouch. Most of the people in the meeting had filed out by then, so it was just me and two other people doing a post-meeting chat. The other person in the room chuckled in agreement. I'd heard this type of comment often at this organization over the two-plus years I had been consulting there. This time it hit different, though, so I countered:

"You know, every time you say that, you perpetuate exactly the type of culture you are currently complaining about. You are describing a part of the culture that should be in the past, but each time you mention it, you drag it into the present day and help move it forward. It's not helping."

Since I had built trust, shown empathy, and (I hope) proven that I knew what I was talking about, my counterpoint landed softly and caused a moment of pause. The two people who remained in the room looked to the side for a few seconds, processing this idea, then looked back at me and nodded. "That's true," they both said, "But…" I don't recall exactly where that next sentence went, but I'm pretty sure it targeted someone else.

Another one of the dumb things our brains do is jump to conclusions and assign blame to other people, before understanding the context of a given situation.

As surely as culture eats strategy, blame kills trust.

Have you ever been driving down the road and been forced to swerve to the side or hit your brakes because of another driver? Of course you have—we've all been there. If your brain immediately thought, *What a jerk!*, then you experienced what psychologists call blame bias. Instead of first considering the surrounding circumstances that may have led to the other driver's actions, we jump to the conclusion that they are bad, and we are good. But what if the other driver didn't make the turn because an old lady was using the crosswalk? Now who's the jerk?

Blame bias impacts our workplace interactions more than we realize.

Our minds naturally blame people—without context, without empathy, without understanding. And, research has found, we tend to believe that other people are more likely to have blame bias than we are.

OUR MINDS NATURALLY BLAME PEOPLE—WITHOUT CONTEXT, WITHOUT EMPATHY, WITHOUT UNDERSTANDING. AND, RESEARCH HAS FOUND, WE TEND TO BELIEVE THAT OTHER PEOPLE ARE MORE LIKELY TO HAVE BLAME BIAS THAN WE ARE.

When blame bias infects a workplace, it creates drama, assumptions, and fear. It destroys trust. Then, all that stress and anxiety goes home with us and infects our personal lives, too.

Take a moment to think about all the people you interact with each day in your job. Try to wrap your head around all the times blame bias could surface, and how, all grouped together, each instance becomes part of your culture. A big part of your culture.

Why did someone miss her deadline? Because she's a slacker. Why was the work sloppy? Because he's not smart. Why didn't that manager show up on time to the meeting he called? Because he's an uncaring person and his mother didn't hold him enough.

"Once you're aware of the blame bias, you'll see it everywhere in your life," Lindsay McGregor and Neel Doshi wrote in *Primed to Perform*.[103] "The most powerful personal antidote is to come up with five alternative explanations for the behavior that do not assume a problem with the person."

McGregor and Doshi recommend the REAP model of feedback to start the hard work of "deblaming your life":

- **Remember.** Assume positive intent.

- **Explain.** Think of five scenarios that could explain why.

- **Ask.** Start with listening to the other person.

- **Plan.** Identify the root cause and make a plan together.

"We invest all sorts of energy in hiring the right people and then underestimate the influence of our culture once they arrive," the authors continue.

The question for most people, however, is *What can you do to influence the culture where you work?* First, stop complaining about the culture. Start defending it instead, even when that's difficult. Too often, the faceless company or a stand-in phrase like "this place" is a facade for a complaint that is actually intended for a person. A company or building can't engage with you in working through an issue, but a person can. Mining for conflict, as Lencioni recommended in the previous chapter, and building trust are powerful tools to building a positive culture.[104] And addressing the blame bias that impacts all of us.

Hallway chatter and side conversations undermine an organization's culture. "The meeting after the meeting," as it is known in some workplaces, is where people openly share their real reservations to a leader's new vision. "That's never going to happen here" is an example of how culture eats strategy for breakfast. As Brené Brown has mentioned many times on her *Dare to Lead* podcast about her own organization, "We talk *to* people, not *about* people."[105]

Those opposing viewpoints need to be part of the conference-room discussion instead. It's so simple, yet so powerful. Mine for dissent, ask uncomfortable questions, say hard things. If an entire organization had this capability, think of how much healthier the culture would be.

I have started leading workshops to help people practice these skills in a safe space. It can help alleviate the fear many of us have that leads us to avoid conflict at all costs.

If you work in a culture in which speaking up in a meeting seems risky; if you can't speak truth to power in an open forum; then focus your attention on building your relationship with your supervisor directly, outside of the meetings. The stronger your direct relationship with the boss is, the more likely it will be for you both to serve as allies for one another during the big meetings.

"Do people trust each other?" Sharon Prill says. "If they do, it opens so many avenues."

You can do more to influence the culture where you work, but it does take courage and effort. Here's how to get started:

MAKING IT HAPPEN

If you have ever wished things were different where you work, take a moment to think through that intention. Then take a few minutes and put pen to paper (or fingers to keyboard). Make a list of roses and thorns:

- **Document.** Write down what you like (roses) and don't like (thorns) about the way your team and your organization operate.

- **Circle the opportunities.** Identify the items on your list that you can directly control or potentially influence.

- **Start with one.** Which one of all the possibilities that you captured would be the easiest to act on? Do that.

- **Own your thinking.** Recognize where the blame bias is negatively influencing your personal relationships at work and use the REAP model to "deblame your life."

- **Take the initiative.** Start to defend the culture when co-workers blame "this place" or "that team," and help them understand how they are contributing to the culture they are complaining about.

If you have a truly terrible boss, there is definitely a limit to how much you can move the needle. (We will explore "managing up" in the next chapter.) It's still possible, however, to own what you can and do your part to steer the culture in a new direction.

CHAPTER 15

MANAGING UP AND ACROSS

I think it's important to dispel the myth that you have to have the title to make change.

—MIKE STEHLIK

Bad bosses are real. Early in her career, Jennifer Sizemore remembers working for one particular supervisor who pushed her into uncomfortable territory on a regular basis.

"Most nights I'd go home and cry," Jennifer told me, describing how this boss was a yeller and someone who took credit for others' work—yet somehow was still someone you'd want to go grab a beer with after work.

People leave managers, not companies. Half of Americans have left a job to "get away from their manager at some point in their career," according to one Gallup study.[106] "The manager accounts for at least 70 percent of the variance in employee engagement."

If you like your job and are engaged in the work, there's much less chance that you'll go interview somewhere else, and Jennifer did just that. She decided to turn her work situation around, despite her difficult boss, pushing herself to find new challenges and gaining valuable experience.

She spent seven years as editor-in-chief of MSNBC.com in the 2000s, when the website was rivaling CNN.com for online news audience supremacy. Then she led the communications and marketing team at the Fred Hutchinson Cancer Research Center, before joining Starbucks as a vice president in marketing.

"Are there still days when I get pissed off? Sure," Jennifer says, now serving as Vice President of Communications at Arnold Ventures, a Texas-based philanthropic organization.[107] "Do I go home and cry? No! Are you kidding?"

Jennifer Sizemore

Jennifer says that maybe it's the maturity she's gained from the past fifteen years that allows her to "handle it" now. She looks back at her younger self and sees a different person, one without the perspective and experience that her current self possesses. She's also come to terms with the fact that she just can't know everything.

"Every year I realize I know less," Jennifer says. "I was SO right in my first job. If you think back, the reason you're always angry and über-passionate is you think you're right. You watch the younger people—I recognize it. Now I have confidence that I know who I am. You hate to think you have it only because you lived long enough."

Given that people stay in jobs—or leave them—because of their boss, what can any one of us do in a challenging situation, such as having a boss who makes you go home and cry every night? Unfortunately, you can't magically gain fifteen years of perspective and experience by snapping your fingers. I know people who would like to stay and love their job because they love the organization, the mission, the work, and the rest of the team. But a bad boss or colleague on another team—someone who is difficult to collaborate with and always taking credit for other people's work—leaves them wondering if they might fit better in a different organization.

The traditional hierarchy of power in the workplace, which can be traced back to the time of factory work, makes this even more difficult. Bosses, supervisors, C-suite officers, and shift managers often affect our work experience one way or another. If you're fortunate to have one of the good ones, congratulations, you're in the minority. If, however, your direct supervisor is moody, uncommunicative, confusing, frustrating, or even infuriating, you are not alone.

Having a bad boss can impact your children, too. One study found that controlling, dominating supervisors led to more authoritarian parenting at home. That's a problem, according to Adam Grant, who connected several other studies and found that children of authoritarian parents are more likely to become bullies and befriend bullies, engage in delinquent behaviors like shoplifting and vandalism, have behavioral problems and become depressed, and start smoking, drinking, and using drugs as adolescents.[108]

In this chapter we will address the challenge of "managing" your manager, and "managing" those who don't report to you. I purposely used quote marks around "managing" in the previous sentence because you aren't actually managing any of those people, yet in the parlance of business and consulting, this strategy is called "managing up and across."

Jennifer is one of the smartest, most talented people I know in business, so I wanted to ask her what she has learned about managing people in all directions during her career. With her bright smile and easy laugh, she said that "communication and connection" are essential.

"It starts at home; it starts with your team. You have to respect each other and have each other's back," Jennifer told me, echoing what we just learned about trust and not avoiding conflict. "People would say to me that everybody loved to work for [me]. It's because I care about people. It makes it easier to reach out to other teams. It's important to make those intentional connections. Maybe I'm more intentional now."

Taking ownership of your relationships at work must be intentional. To foster better communication and connection, first consider the assumptions you might be making about your boss, or about frustrating colleagues on another team—you know, the ones who can't seem to reply to your emails or are always missing their deadlines. As we saw in the previous chapter, we must continually battle our "blame bias." Those assumptions, and lack of trust, are the biggest threats to a healthy culture and workplace relationships—and by extension, your work-life happiness.

"Before you act, what assumptions do you make?" asks Jill Geisler, author of *Work Happy: What Great Bosses Know*,[109] and someone I started learning from more than a decade ago, when we both taught at the Poynter Institute in Florida.[110] "If you want a culture of respect and trust, then you have to challenge those assumptions."

People are instinctively myopic, whether they want to admit it or not. It's simply how our brains are wired. We care more about our project or idea than others do, which makes sense, but we often don't recognize that reality.

"The narrative that everyone keeps repeating is that 'no one cares about this or that!' Maybe there are more people who care about this or that than you are giving credit to, but you won't ever know until you stop assuming and start asking questions," Jill told me.

Questions are taken for granted in the workplace, and throughout our human experience, according to Edgar Schein, who has received degrees from the University of Chicago, Harvard, and Stanford, and served as professor emeritus at MIT.[111] His research and teachings in the area of workplace culture have influenced generations of managers and consultants. He found, time and again, that what solves problems, what moves things forward, is asking the right questions, a practice he termed Humble Inquiry.

 **BUTTERFLY IMPACT SIGNPOST**

"Humble Inquiry is the fine art of drawing someone out, of asking questions to which you do not already know the answer, of building a relationship based on curiosity and interest in the other person," Schein wrote in his 2013 book, appropriately titled *Humble Inquiry: The Gentle Art of Asking Instead of Telling*. "Ultimately the purpose of Humble Inquiry is to build relationships that lead to trust which, in turn, leads to better communication and collaboration."

How we relate to other human beings is not given formal treatment in school, nor is it part of the typical onboarding process at work. Yet it impacts our happiness at work and engagement in our jobs more than almost anything else. You may have noticed that relationship challenges keep surfacing in this book. The relationship you have with your boss, or those who don't report to you, will go a long way to determining how much of that work-life happiness you experience on a regular basis.

Schein recommends "here-and-now humility": recognizing the need to ask questions and seek help from others when facing a task at work, especially a challenging one. It's the difference between young Jennifer Sizemore—who was sure she was so right—and mature Jennifer Sizemore, who understands that every year she knows less.

CHART A PATH FORWARD

Marissa Nelson has spent the past two decades as a manager and director at multiple news operations in Canada. She remembers a time when she made the effort to learn—and teach—that really paid off. During one particularly challenging and stressful period, Marissa's "boss's boss" (one level above her boss) had "a lot of opinions about the minutiae of my operation."

These opinions would hit Marissa in the form of emails, hallway chats, or through her direct supervisor. She would be asked why one thing or another was—or was not—happening. Marissa says they were really small details for a very senior leader to be worrying about.

"Frankly, these issues were below what *I* should have been dealing with!" says Marissa, whose energy, wit, and colorful language are infectious.[112] We met more than fifteen years ago at a seminar for new leaders at the Poynter Institute in Florida, and I've been laughing with—and learning from—Marissa ever since. "[The questions] always came with a sense of urgency, and that urgency would send me and my team into a tailspin—pushing our day off course and our focus off."

It was also an increasing issue for Marissa's boss, who was fielding these questions as well, often blindsided by a complaint from that same boss above him.

"And then it suddenly dawned on me: we were all having these entirely transactional conversations about tactical things, and as long as I engaged in the conversation I was making the situation worse," Marissa told me. "I was aiding the constant circling of the drain. I mustered up the courage to talk directly to my boss about the issue, and charted out a path forward."

Marissa Nelson

In the spirit of Humble Inquiry, Marissa asked her boss questions to get to the root of the issue. She then built a detailed, written strategy for this one part of the operation. The document would help her boss guide other stakeholders back to the substantive issues and, hopefully, create buy-in for the direction in which Marissa and her team wanted to take the business. She worked with her top lieutenant to create a three-page document to present to her boss, and then asked more questions. She then incorporated the feedback and input.

"We squirreled ourselves away for a day and charted out the future," Marissa says. "I'm not sure it got the buy-in up the chain I'd hoped for, but it certainly armed my boss with information, and the constant bombardment and criticism did abate."

The time and effort invested helped shore up a "trust wobble" between her and those above her on the org chart.

Managing across is just as important. Especially when you need to influence someone in another department or another team. How do you "tell them what to do" without telling them what to do? *Because nobody likes being told what to do.*

Mike Stehlik

Mike Stehlik knows about managing across teams in a complex organization. He has spent fifteen years navigating the inner workings of the Securities and Exchange Commission (SEC) in the US Federal Government. With more than 4,000 lawyers, accountants, and analysts spread across five divisions, the challenge of cross-collaboration is daunting.

Mike (who was my backcourt running mate on our college intramural basketball team) works in the Division of Corporation Finance, which investigates fraud and malfeasance by US companies. The SEC organizational chart used to include more than a half dozen different levels of reporting. This meant a lot of bosses and supervisors. The commission recently worked to flatten out the number of levels, Mike says, with the goal of reducing the overall number of managers. This created an opportunity—and a need—for leading without authority.

"I thought it was really powerful when I heard that," says Mike.[113] "Leading without formal delegated authority gives you a bit of attitude when you walk in and say, 'Hey, I don't have the title, but here's the plan.' [Once] I would have gone to my boss to make this decision, but now I don't. I just make it. You feel empowered when you can take control of your destiny."

In addition to empowerment, according to Keith Ferrazzi, leading without authority can also create more engagement and more meaning in your work. Ferrazzi, who published a book titled *Leading Without Authority* in 2020, is also the bestselling author of *Who's Got Your Back* and *Never Eat Alone,* and has spent his career helping teams work together more effectively.[114] The cornerstone of this approach is something Ferrazzi calls co-elevation, defined as "going higher together." Co-elevation means turning colleagues into teammates, nurturing "generosity of spirit" and a sense of commitment to a shared mission. And it can help add to your team of allies at work.

To identify that "shared mission," Ferrazzi recommends identifying the "blue flame" in your teammates or colleagues. "The blue flame is what gives our lives meaning; it's what we value most—our purpose, our passion, our calling. It's the aspiration that lives deep inside us. And when this blue flame is ignited within someone, it's what makes them bounce out of bed in the morning, eager to make a difference in the world."

How do you find someone's blue flame? Start with Humble Inquiry, of course. Listening is a practice and a skill that can be taught, learned, and practiced. Becoming a better listener is required for realizing the full power of The Butterfly Impact because, as we've seen, so much of our work-life happiness revolves around our relationships at work. When you take the time and make the effort to ask questions and listen to your teammates, to learn their story and know them as people instead of simply co-workers, it makes every challenge you face together easier to tackle.

"I think it's important to dispel the myth that you have to have the title to make change," Mike told me. "If you are building trust, building beneficial partnerships, that's how you have influence over the people above you and around you."

Managing up and across is a skill that is rarely taught or trained, yet it can make or break your experience at work. Here's how to go about it.

ASK QUESTIONS TO LEARN HOW YOUR BOSS WANTS TO BE COMMUNICATED TO.

MANAGING UP AND ACROSS: START WITH QUESTIONS

Understanding how others like to work and matching your communication style to conform to their preferences can make a big difference. Be overt and intentional in asking specific questions:

- How your boss wants to be communicated to. Formally with scheduled meetings or informally with impromptu check-ins?

- How much detail do you feel you need to know about what's going on? Is what I've [you've] been providing too much or too little? Has it been in the right form? Which do you prefer: frequent short updates or a scheduled weekly roundup?

Again, use Humble Inquiry to engage your boss and each of your colleagues. Ask them:

- What is important to you? What are your goals, at work and in life? How can I [you] help achieve those goals?

There's a good chance they may never have considered these questions, and they will help create engagement between you in your work relationship.

There's also a chance they are just as afraid to address these questions as you are. A 2016 Harris poll of 1,120 employed US workers revealed that the fear goes both ways: 69 percent of managers are just as afraid of communication as their teams.[115] It's important to have empathy for your boss and colleagues, too.

"'How are [you] judged, evaluated, considered successful?'" Jill Geisler recommends asking your supervisor and teammates these fundamental questions. "'What irritates [you] without even knowing it?' Find out what pressures they're under."

"Ask them, 'Who's the best boss you've ever worked for? Who treated you in a way you thought was terrific?'"

This same approach will work well with your teammates and even those you manage.

This only works, of course, if you really listen to your boss and teammates. These one-on-one conversations, according to Jill, will help form a bond and common understanding that will pay dividends in your relationships at work—and your work-life happiness—over time.

MAKING IT HAPPEN

If you have an especially difficult person at work, managing up and across will be one of the most challenging aspects of improving work-life happiness. Here are a few ways to tackle it.

- **Practice Humble Inquiry before using it in your workplace.** Identify a safe relationship in which you can test the waters with a small experiment. Maybe it's with a personal friend, a spouse or partner, or even a work friend whom you know well. How many questions can you ask (without being annoying)?

- **Know how your boss and teammates want to communicate.** Ask how they communicate with their boss and model your methods to their preferences.

- **Know the threshold at which your boss wants to be informed or involved.** Is what you've been doing too much or not enough? That will make any boss happier.

- **Find out what makes a great day at work for your teammates.** Managing across can be more challenging than managing up. Use Humble Inquiry to learn as much as you can about the duties, tasks, and stresses of those in other work groups. Look for situations where you feel people are making unreasonable demands, then spend some time walking in their shoes.

One final note on the frustration you likely feel facing the challenges associated with managing up and across: If you need to vent, think through where that's coming from, and whom you can talk with in confidence. Remember, you are the culture.

CHAPTER 16

BUILD TRUST WITH BETTER FEEDBACK

It's not what you say, but how you say it.
—DAVE SMITH

Eight minutes and forty-six seconds.

Do you remember when you first saw the video of George Floyd being murdered? His face in pain, being crushed against the asphalt by one police officer while three others observed nearby. His cries for help. "I can't breathe. I can't breathe."

People of a certain generation talk about where they were when they heard Kennedy had been shot. Or Reagan. My generation had 9/11. This generation has George Floyd, who wasn't famous at the time of his death, but whose cruel killing established a moment in history that reverberated indelibly around the world.

Three days after Floyd's murder, Porsha Grant sent an email

to a newsroom distribution list at the Philadelphia TV station where she worked at the time. As a Black woman and a manager, Porsha felt someone needed to address the oversized elephant in the room. The subject line: "Racial Trauma." In it, she wrote:

I'm just going to say it. I'm tired.

If your social media feeds look like mine, you'll see that a lot of Black people are feeling this way. There's always an undercurrent of these feelings, I think. But between the Central Park incident and George Floyd…mix in a little COVID-19 and the disparities it has shone a light on…and…yeah, people are tired. Angry, and tired.[116]

Her email went on to ask, "How about finding a mental health expert to address this?" Before HR or company leaders could respond to the situation, Porsha found herself filling that need.

"I guess it took somebody to break the ice," Porsha told me. "It was just a short little email saying 'Yo, this is heavy. This is how I feel. If you have friends or know people that look like me, they are probably feeling the same way.' I felt like that kind of broke the ice, because people just started responding, and responding, and responding."

Once the ice had been broken, a conversation emerged, first by email, then in person. "People said, 'I have some questions; can you help me with these questions?' Porsha remembers. "Nobody wants to be the representative of one's race, right? Because we are not a monolith. None of us are. But people felt more comfortable in saying, 'I've got some questions. I've never experienced that. What can I do? I don't know what to say. What can I say?'"

While it took a little prodding, once the conversations started happening—and happening within earshot of other people—people who had been hesitant to speak up were more comfortable in having those conversations, Porsha recalls.

Difficult conversations build trust. The more we trust someone, the easier it becomes to have difficult conversations. It becomes a virtuous circle. Difficult conversations can be uncomfortable, but growth can only happen once we step outside our comfort zone.

DIFFICULT CONVERSATIONS BUILD TRUST

The more we trust someone, the easier it becomes to have difficult conversations.

It takes leadership to kick-start those conversations. Leadership comes naturally to Porsha, something she recognized early in her career. With an affinity for writing, she found her way into journalism and TV news at the University of Georgia. In her first internship, she discovered the job role of producer as someone who called the shots. That appealed to her.

"I saw the producer was the boss of the newscast, and I thought, I like...bossing," Porsha says with a laugh. "I can do that."

Following graduation, she started working in TV news in Augusta, then Charlotte. Her ambition drove her desire for an opportunity in an even bigger market. Yet, she wanted to stay in the Southeast, close to home and able to drive to her mom's house for Sunday dinner on occasion.

Then a recruiter sent her resume to 6ABC in Philadelphia, one of the top TV stations in one of the biggest markets in the US. Despite the job being farther from home than she had planned, Porsha felt compelled to give it a shot. She still remembers crying tears of anxiety and uncertainty as she faxed the signed letter from Kinko's to officially accept the job. And commit to moving her life to the Northeast.

Porsha Grant

Her ambition and leadership skills continued to drive her forward. In fifteen years at the Philadelphia station, she has produced pretty much everything. In the fall of 2020, ABC tapped her to lead a new Race and Culture team for its eight TV stations across the nation.

It was around this time, a few months removed from the George Floyd tragedy, when I had the privilege of working with Porsha; the assistant news director at the station, Christine Bowley; and my consulting colleague, John Culliton, on four internal sessions for station personnel that we called "Crucial Conversations." The sessions were optional and, due to the pandemic, held through video calls. About ten to fifteen people joined for each session to continue the discussion that Porsha had sparked with that email back in May. In the final session, nearly everyone broke down in tears at one point or another. Including me. Porsha talked about her journey in a poor family in Georgia, a single generation removed from sharecroppers, and how she had been told her whole life that she would have to do everything "twice as good for half the credit." One of Porsha's colleagues talked about his son not getting invited to his best friend's birthday party because he was Black. A young Black-Asian reporter detailed how she struggled with double racism growing up because she was seen as neither Black nor Asian by those groups. And a white manager spoke about the racism he had seen in his own friends toward his Asian wife.

The topic of "how has racism impacted you" created an out-pouring of openness and emotion. The catharsis felt immensely powerful, even over a video call. The openness, honesty, and candor people showed up with can be traced back to the email Porsha sent in May. Difficult conversations build trust. Trust makes difficult conversations easier. Each event increases the positive effect of the next—another example of how The Butter-fly Impact can ripple throughout a team or organization.

BUTTERFLY IMPACT SIGNPOST

Trust is the cornerstone of a healthy (and happy) work life. Trust allows you to expose assumptions, have difficult conversations, challenge one another, and offer and receive better feedback. Trust replaces stress and anxiety; rather than worrying what your boss is thinking or why she made this decision, you trust her to have the organization's best interests in mind. If needed, you can ask direct questions and know that she will understand that you also have the organization's best interests in mind.

While 2020 brought many challenges, one silver lining is a collective reckoning that we needed to get better at having conversations on race and diversity as well as mental and emotional health. Those are *really* difficult conversations. As I watched courageous people open up in front of their colleagues that year, I couldn't help but think how much easier it could be to talk about work stuff in the future.

"It took an extra level of comfort for me to go into how I feel like I'm carrying the weight of the generations before me," Porsha told me. "And how I want to make them proud that their sacrifices and the discrimination and their daily struggle and what they went through…was not in vain. Because I took that and built upon it…I'm going to pass it on to my children and keep it going."

When you trust someone, you can say hard things. And ask tough questions. You can also offer direct and constructive feedback on performance, ideas, and other work-related issues.

Why is feedback so hard? Because we are all self-conscious creatures who constantly worry what others are thinking about us. Plus, we naturally turn defensive the moment we sense negative feedback, like a boxer cornered in the ring. Studies show that people unconsciously drift away from co-workers who are known to offer criticism or negative feedback. We find our way to those people who build us up, are "safe" and friendly.

Feedback, of course, is how we get better. Yet feedback conversations on work performance have always been difficult. Since feedback is a process to foster improvement, how will you ever get better, if you never actually hear the feedback?

One way that many people have experienced feedback and criticism is the "feedback sandwich," that classic feedback delivery system in which you start with some small praise, follow it with criticism, and top it off with more praise. The idea is that people will be more open to the criticism if you lead with something positive. It's such a well-known method that Meg Peters, who has spent more than seven years working at Facebook, says there's a joke among her friends about having a "straight deli meat kind of day." This happens when it feels like all the feedback is criticism and none of it is praise. All meat and no bread. She started her career as a newspaper reporter and quickly grew accustomed to feedback early on: an editor would mark up each of her news articles and suggest areas for improvement, making it a constant part of the culture. It's similar at Facebook, she says. And trust is a key part of the process.

Meg Peters

"Especially when the stakes are so high," Meg says, acknowledging how much focus in 2020 fell on Facebook in the midst of the election, the pandemic, and the Black Lives Matter movement.[117] "We work at such a scale that getting to that level of trust is really, really important."

As trust grows, honest feedback becomes easier and more effective. It is another virtuous cycle: More trust leads to more, and better, feedback. More frequent feedback leads to more trust. And so on.

"I've personally benefited from a lot of the team building we do at Facebook," Meg says. "Having that common bond is the first building block of trust, and as you work more closely together over time, the trust starts to come more easily as you have more and more shared experiences. Trust helps you develop that openness, so you don't immediately recoil when that harsher feedback comes."

Meg contributed to one of my earlier books on digital journalism, way back in 2012, when she worked as a community manager for the social media website Mashable. Spending more than a decade working on the front lines of social media and news has given her a unique view into how *not* to offer—or receive—feedback. No one wants to see their workplace culture turn into the cesspool that most comment sections on the internet are—perfect examples of feedback without trust.

Trust during the feedback process is also necessary because, let's face it, we are all fragile creatures. Feedback threatens to activate the "impostor syndrome" inside us. Two American psychologists coined the term in 1978 to describe the feeling of "phoniness in people who believe that they are not intelligent, capable or creative despite evidence of high achievement." Pauline Clance and Suzanne Imes found that people who "are highly motivated to achieve," also often "live in fear of being 'found out' or exposed as frauds."[118]

I assume most people struggle with this—I battle it daily. I spent months trying to fully convince myself that I was capable of writing the book you are currently reading. I'm not sure that self-doubt ever goes away.

In addition to building trust with the people at your job, what are some other ways you can help create a culture of constructive feedback? Here are some specific steps to get you started.

MAKING IT HAPPEN

- **Ask for advice rather than feedback.** A team of Harvard researchers found that people received more effective input from colleagues when they asked for "advice" rather than "feedback."[119] By initiating these conversations with teammates, you will also be flattering them with your (I hope sincere) respect for their opinion, and creating new paths for dialogue and trust-building.

- **Find a feedback partner.** Find someone friendly who will give you feedback on a recent project or presentation, then reciprocate. In the beginning, keep it fun and light as you build trust with one another. You will instinctively be developing language that you can use when offering feedback to others in the future.

- **Give yourself a second score.** You probably work with people who are "coachable." You can make a suggestion, and they will appreciate it. Have you thought about how coachable *you* are? Adam Grant recommends something he calls a "second score" to gauge your own coachability.

"Every time I get feedback, I rate myself now on how well I took the feedback," Grant says.[120] "That's a habit we can all develop. When someone gives you feedback, they've already evaluated you. So, it helps to remind yourself that the main thing they're judging now is whether you're open or defensive. You don't always realize when you're being defensive."

"It's not what you say, but how you say it" is the advice Dave Smith offered me when I started my consulting career at SmithGeiger in 2017.[121] The substance of the feedback, input, or advice is one part of the equation. But the manner in which it's delivered is even more important. That's how trust is built. Or destroyed.

Porsha remembers one manager who had a habit of making people feel stupid. Maybe you've had one of these in your life, too? Your ideas don't just get shot down. You also feel belittled.

"Long term, you don't want to say anything," Porsha says. "I got mad, and eventually decided I'm going to say what I want to say anyway. I learned that, as a manager, that's what I didn't want to be."

CHAPTER 17

WORK SHOULD BE FUN AND, SOMETIMES, FUNNY

"Rats stop laughing if they feel anxious."

—SOPHIE SCOTT

Jen Lee Reeves has a loud, infectious laugh that can light up a room and make you feel a rush of warmth. She sees a world of endless possibilities for joy, a celebration of the human spirit, and the human experience.

She also works harder than almost anyone I know.

Until recently, Jen was working as Director of Digital Communications at the University of Missouri, where she led strategic planning and brand consistency for the school online. In 2020, Jen decided to focus fully on her communications consultancy.

She always has at least one side project going and sees opportunities everywhere, even in places where others might not. She simply has too much positive energy and enthusiasm to limit herself, and has a clear direction for how she wants to spend her time and spread her gifts.

"I can't function on a daily basis without joy," Jen told me.[122] "My entire career has been steered toward joy. It impacts everything—who I hire, who I married. Everything."

In 2005, Jen started blogging. At first, she wrote about work-related topics in digital media, but when her daughter Jordan was born without a full left arm (it stops after the humerus), Jen shifted the focus of the blog. Her stories of parenting a child born with a physical difference became a book, then a nonprofit foundation helping kids and parents around the globe. The organization's mission is to build creative solutions that help kids with differences live a more enjoyable life. Jen and Jordan's work has evolved into a movement and has been featured on *The Today Show* and other media nationwide. The book, *Born Just Right*, won Digital Book World's Best Children's Book award in 2019. Jordan was a finalist for *TIME* Magazine's Kid of the Year in 2020.[123]

Jen says her work with Jordan on the blog (after more than 1,500 posts), the book, and the foundation has always been "centered on joy and not making assumptions." She feels blessed to work with so many people who are proud of who they are instead of focusing on who they are not.

"We all get it because we are joyful for it," Jen told me. "It's nothing to be sad about. When someone would see Jordan when she was younger and say, 'Awww' [and express sadness for her difference], I think it's too bad they don't take a moment to learn something. If someone was making assumptions, then I'm sad for them."

Jen Lee Reeves

Make no mistake, Jen is rarely sad. She brings joy and laughter to every aspect of her varied and successful career, in addition to all her passion projects on the side. I met Jen many years ago when our paths kept crossing at the same industry conferences, including SXSW Interactive, which brings tens of thousands to Austin, Texas. After wrapping up for the day, we met up with some others on Rainey Street, an Austin hot spot. Knowing Jen, I was certain I would find smiles, jokes, and the kind of laughter that doubles you over and makes you slap the table. And I was right.

"I come to joy naturally. And I consider it a privilege. I'm very fortunate to be that way," Jen told me.

Infusing laughter and joy into her work makes her ten-, twelve-, and fourteen-hour days possible. And usually fun. It's not for everyone, though, unfortunate as that may be.

"I tend to lightly say something in meetings for a laugh, try to keep things light," Jen says. "One time a leader came into a meeting and she was kinda new, and I said something to her I thought was funny, but I didn't realize she was the most literal human in the universe. She looked at me and I thought, *Oh crap. There's no way I'm ever going to be able to loosen up the room with her. She's just not fun.* That's one way to figure it out pretty quickly!"

 **BUTTERFLY IMPACT SIGNPOST**

Laughter has been proven to lighten your load mentally, enhance your intake of oxygen-rich air, release endorphins in your brain, aid muscle relaxation, and reduce stress. Despite the physiological benefits of laughter, our workplace culture—born in the era of factories and poisoned by the constant pressure of potential layoffs in the push for quarterly profits—has rarely made it a priority.

Andrew Tarvin is trying to change that. In 2012 Tarvin launched a company called Humor That Works and, in 2019, published a book by the same name.[124] He and his team have helped more than 25,000 people from 250 organizations around the world use humor to achieve success and happiness in the workplace. One of his biggest learnings has been that humor is not a one-time event. It's not something you learn from a single talk, and not something you benefit from by doing a single time.

"The real benefits come when humor becomes a habit, when it

becomes part of how you get things done," Tarvin writes. I love this concept: that humor can become a habit just like brushing your teeth, eating a healthy snack, or regular exercise.

With more than 700 blog posts, a "database of office humor," hundreds of ways to use humor at work, and actual lists of jokes, Tarvin's website is quite a resource. Some of the jokes you'll find there:

- I always tell new hires, don't think of me as your boss, think of me as a friend who can fire you.

- The proper way to use a stress ball is to throw it at the last person to upset you.

- Knowledge is knowing a tomato is a fruit; wisdom is not putting it in a fruit salad.

- Keep the dream alive: hit the snooze button.

I'll be honest: I've read Tarvin's book and gone through his website and watched his talks and rarely laughed out loud. That's not the point, however. Incorporating humor at work isn't about becoming the next Jim Gaffigan or Chris Rock to entertain the people you work with. It's a discipline and a process that brings surprise and delight into the daily grind. It's relieving the pressure of work and making it okay to have fun while you play the game of business.

In my work, I see teams in different organizations interact with one another. I see how the dynamic can change dramatically if a certain person is, or isn't, in a meeting. In my experience, the more laughter, the more humor, the stronger the culture and the team. These are also the top-performing teams I work with, the kind who adapt quickly to new challenges and quickly come together to solve problems (and routinely achieve their goals and hit their numbers).

The people on these teams are also happier and more fulfilled, of course, which is what The Butterfly Impact is all about. What are the stories you tell your friend or spouse or partner about your day at work: The meeting that efficiently covered objectives and KPIs with information-packed charts and graphs? Or the meeting when your boss led her presentation with a funny clip of Chandler and Joey from *Friends* that had the whole room smiling?

One of the best practitioners of bringing lightness and unstructured humor into the workplace is Wendy McMahon, the former president of ABC Owned Television Stations. She convinced my current employer to create a new role in 2017 to help her transform the organization through extensive modernization efforts, and that's been my job ever since. She spends her days in one potentially stressful meeting after another; yet no matter how serious or dire the topic of conversation, Wendy can find a way to smile and make you smile, too. She's lucky, because it comes easy for her.

"For the most part, I don't consciously make those decisions to bring lightness into difficult moments," Wendy told me.[125] "It's typically inspired or guided by the belief that everyone involved in the conversation has good intentions and believes in the purpose and value of what we're doing."

Remember when I said that you are the culture? That's especially true if you are the boss. You can set the tone for an entire organization. I had the privilege of watching Wendy influence an organization of more than 1,600 employees. Whether consciously or not, she was reflecting a culture developed by Bob Iger, the former Disney CEO and her former boss, who is a master at disarming a room—or a global video call with thousands of employees—with a joke and laughter, often at his own expense.

"Confronting stressful topics and situations is necessary, but your brain is always going to do its best work if it doesn't feel threatened and/or defensive," Wendy says. "So, lightening the mood is in service to the desire to drive healthy dialogue that arrives at a solution or a next step. I also think keeping things light enables innovation and freedom to create."

"Rats stop laughing if they feel anxious," according to Sophie Scott, a neuroscientist and professor at University College London. "Humans do the same thing." *Yes, it turns out rats laugh. Look it up.*

It makes sense that laughter helps us cope with stress. It also builds trust, forges bonds among colleagues, and inspires creativity and problem-solving, according to Bruce Daisley, a former Twitter vice president and author of *Eat Sleep Work Repeat: 30 Hacks for Bringing Joy to Your Job*. "In short, laughter is the secret weapon for building great teams," Daisley wrote in the book.[126] Teams who laugh and joke together tend to be better able to open up and share challenges with each other.

The Mayo Clinic says laughter can also make it easier to cope with difficult situations, and helps you connect with other people.[127] Laughter is disarming. When a leader delivers challenging news to her team and follows with a self-deprecating comment and a chuckle or laughter, the stress level on the team comes down a notch.

Can one joke make a meaningful difference in how people are viewed by others? In a controlled study, the answer was unequivocally yes.[128] Participants who heard one presenter make a statement with a joke at the end rated that presenter as more confident and more competent than they did another presenter who made the same statement without the joke. The researchers noted that "the jokey presenter was also more likely to be voted as the leader for subsequent group tasks."

With all this research confirming what most of us already intuitively understand, why isn't humor at work more prevalent? For one thing, it can be risky, and requires a level of vulnerability that is uncomfortable for some people. What if the joke falls flat? Or accidentally offends someone? It's also extra work in a time-starved day; finding the right meme to insert into your presentation, or taking another minute to craft a witty email reply, takes time and energy. Often it's just easier to play it straight.

Prioritizing humor and laughter at work is worth the time and energy, however. And it will pay dividends to you, your team, and the people in your life outside of work, who will get to experience a less-stressed, happier individual.

MAKING IT HAPPEN

How do you get more laughter in your life? It just takes a little effort and intention. For example:

- Identify the joy in what you do, and be intentional in bringing joy to the work, the meetings, the Zoom calls, and other interactions.

- Search for funny memes (or ask your teenager for some, if you have one—that's my trick, anyway) and share them with your team. Bonus points if you can share them with your boss! If that's not possible yet because your boss will think you're slacking in your work, ask your boss to read this chapter.

- Start meetings at work or conversations with friends and family by cracking a joke at your own expense. Self-deprecating humor is effective and safe. Even if you're not naturally funny, laughing at yourself makes it OK for others to laugh, too.

- Before heading into a group situation, watch standup comedy on Netflix or another streaming service, or listen to comedy stations on Pandora or Spotify. If you show up after laughing hysterically, the positive energy will spill over into the room and become infectious. You don't even have to remember any of the jokes. (This works for social situations, too.)

The research behind the positive impact of humor is overwhelming. And it just makes sense. Even people who are naturally more serious or introverted (like the leader in Jen's earlier story) can benefit from the positive energy in an environment that includes laughter and smiling. As Wendy pointed out, it creates a safer space for freedom and creativity.

Plus, it feels good to laugh and find joy—*really* good. And there's no reason not to do more of it, even if you're at work—especially if you're at work.

CHAPTER 18

BE GRATEFUL. AND ON TIME.

"Life would've been pretty bad for us if we had experienced a similar pandemic."
—T'WINA NOBLES

Appreciation and gratitude are simple, free, and available to everyone.

T'wina Nobles is someone who doesn't take anything for granted. As a child, she suffered years of abuse and homelessness, moving from one shelter to the next; at one point she was completely on her own, without any family. She was eventually moved into the foster care system in Alabama yet, somehow, put her life together.

Actually, she did more than that. When I met her in 2020, I had trouble wrapping my head around everything she had going on: CEO of the Tacoma [Washington] Urban League, school board member, leader of a non-profit called Ladies First to mentor young girls, and a mother of four children.

Given her passion for community involvement, people had started encouraging her a few years ago to run for office. T'wina hadn't warmed to the idea, in part due to everything else on her plate—until one day in March 2020. She had scheduled a meeting with the state senator who represented her district (and mine) to discuss issues related to her work for the Urban League. The state senator didn't shown up to meet with her group.

"I remember being really excited to meet him and talk about the Urban League," T'wina told me.[129] "People had been spreading rumors that I was going to challenge him in the fall, and I was thinking at some point (in the meeting) I would say, 'Don't worry, I'm not going to run.'"

T'wina Nobles

She never got that chance and, following the no-show, T'wina filed the necessary paperwork and started assembling her team. Campaigning as a newcomer against a two-term incumbent—in the midst of the pandemic and stay-at-home restrictions—presented a steep challenge. No doorbelling. No fundraising events to stage. No Kiwanis breakfasts or chamber lunches to speak to. T'wina and her team managed to meet the moment, seizing the energy from the Black Lives Matter movement that gave T'wina a stage, even when it was over Zoom. She surprised many when she won the primary in September by a few hundred votes. That led state and national party fundraisers to bolster her opponent with new infusions of cash (and attack ads) in an attempt to hold on to the seat. In November she won in a narrow race with 50.6 percent of the votes. She is now the only Black senator in the state of Washington.

"Him not coming to that meeting—honestly I felt disappointed," T'wina says. "It made me feel not represented, and feel for all those people who are not feeling represented."

The year 2020 taught us all many lessons, maybe none more important than to stop taking things in our life for granted—and above all, to be grateful for what we have, especially if we made it through the year safe, healthy, and employed.

"This year I became especially grateful for stability, specifically, housing security," T'wina said at the end of 2020. "I found myself reflecting on the many times our family would be walking up and down streets seeking food or housing as children. Life would've been pretty bad for us if we had experienced a similar pandemic [then]."

 BUTTERFLY IMPACT SIGNPOST

Books, articles, and research on the powerful benefits of gratitude have exploded in recent years. While still limited, research on gratitude in the workplace has linked it to more positive emotions, less stress, fewer health complaints and sick days, and higher satisfaction with jobs and co-workers.[130] In short, gratitude is another powerful tool in your toolbox for building work-life happiness and leveraging The Butterfly Impact.

Research has found that people wish they were thanked more often at work, while they also admit they were less likely to express gratitude themselves at work compared to other parts of their life. And therein lies the problem. Good leaders already do this. My favorite example is the former Campbell's Soup CEO who wrote 30,000 thank-you notes to his employees.[131] It makes my hand hurt just thinking about it. Whether you're a CEO or a front-line staffer, you can make a difference in your work life by actively practicing and expressing gratitude regularly.

Appreciation is the point of this chapter. When appreciation takes the form of gratitude, it helps you recognize the successes, opportunities, and positive relationships you have at work. Gratitude helps you focus your appreciation beyond yourself and leads you to recognize that other people play a role in your positive outcomes at work.

Beyond writing thousands of thank-you notes, what can any individual do to channel the powerful benefit of gratitude in the workplace? Get involved and give back.

T'wina remembers two teachers who inspired her to do just that. One woman, Miss Miles, ran one of the shelters she lived in as a child. "She was this Black woman, really gorgeous, running an organization and had this large desk in her office," T'wina says. "She was graceful and poised and, because of her, I saw myself as an executive someday."

The other woman inspired T'wina to become a youth coach before starting the nonprofit organization, Ladies First. She organizes and leads field trips for young girls and outings to Mount Rainier, sailing on Puget Sound, or hiking in the Olympic National Forest.

"I became a coach for ten years because I wanted to be like them, to have that impact in my community," T'wina says. "People need to see someone doing it. They need to be inspired by someone."

Could that be you? Most companies do some form of giving back nowadays, but those efforts are often invisible or unfelt by most employees. You can change that by organizing an effort to bring your teammates together to give back to the community where you work. The vast majority of Americans say they would prefer to work for a company that supports charitable causes when they are deciding between two jobs with the same location, responsibilities, pay, and benefits.

"Over and over I have seen that when people feel they are all working together to help others, office morale is high, and negative office politics don't tend to develop," says Blake Mycoskie. "This creates wonderful working conditions and helps attract and retain loyal employees."

As the Chief Shoe Giver at TOMS Shoes, the company he founded in 2006, Mycoskie knows more than most about giving back. He pioneered the One for One program, which has now provided roughly 100 million pairs of shoes to people in need. TOMS employees and volunteers travel to developed nations to perform "shoe drops" to hand-deliver the shoes. The photos on the company website, and in Mycoskie's book, *Start Something That Matters*, are inspiring.[132]

Studies show that grateful employees are more concerned about social responsibility, according to the Greater Good Science Center at the University of California, Berkeley. Grateful employees—as well as employees who receive more gratitude—also perform more "organizational citizenship" behaviors: kind acts that aren't part of their job description, like welcoming new employees and filling in for co-workers.

Building a culture of giving back naturally leads to a culture of appreciation and gratitude. I worked for one company that participated in the Adopt-A-Highway program. We would don bright orange vests and pick up trash along a strip of road near our office. And other strange items. *It's a little disturbing what people will throw out of their car.* At another job, I actually looked forward to the first Saturday in December and the opportunity to stand outside on a dark, cold, rainy morning to help with an annual food drive. I would even drag my kids along, too. They didn't love it as much as I did, but it's amazing how far a little hot chocolate and donuts will go.

The glow from good deeds like these burns for days, even weeks, afterward. Interactions with co-workers feel different, better. You can make this happen. If you work primarily on a team of five people, for example, volunteer with your group at the local food pantry once a month. It really doesn't take much time and effort, but the rewards are exponential.

When you do an act that feels like giving back, you're more likely to appreciate everything else in your life.

WHEN YOU DO AN ACT THAT FEELS LIKE GIVING BACK, YOU'RE MORE LIKELY TO APPRECIATE EVERYTHING ELSE IN YOUR LIFE.

One study in the *Journal of Business Ethics* found that employees with stronger feelings of hope and gratitude had a greater sense of responsibility toward employee and societal issues.[133] Meaning you should get your boss involved, too. If you can, maybe he or she will *appreciate you more*. Gratitude is a powerful form of feedback, and more managers should take advantage.[134]

Feedback is hard. Saying thank you is easier and almost always appreciated.

The more specific the thanks, the higher the quality. While any form of thanks is better than none at all, be granular with your gratitude for full effect. It feels different to be told thank you for something specific and why the person is grateful for you and your actions. Make the extra effort to do it well.

On a personal level, dozens of research studies found that gratitude will make you happier, healthier, help you sleep better, boost your self-esteem and your career. No other simple act has been found to be so powerful.

Gratitude and giving back are both forms of appreciation and run counter to the trap of taking things for granted. Another way to do this is to simply be on time—to meetings, to calls, and anywhere else you said you'd be at a certain time. When you arrive five or ten minutes late to a work or personal meeting, you are taking the person who showed up on time for granted. The more people waiting for you, the more selfish this is.

There are obviously times when running late can't be avoided, and everyone understands that. Then there are those people who consistently arrive late to meetings and calls. This message is for you: stop. Chronic late-arrivers cause stress for those who are waiting for them. This is the opposite of a healthy organizational culture or work-life happiness.

There is research that suggests late people are actually less stressed because they are less concerned about being late. That disregards the social contract those late people make—and break—each time they show up several minutes after a meeting or call is scheduled to start. Just as a legal contract clearly stipulates what each party will give and receive, this social contract should feel binding. You agreed to a specific start time when you accepted the calendar invitation. Honor it.

MAKING IT HAPPEN

- **Thank the people who never get thanked.** Every organization has people who work behind the scenes. Their efforts make it possible for the organization to succeed and for others to bask in the spotlight of accomplishment. Identify those people and thank them for the little things they do to make others' work lives better.

- **The Appreciation Hot Seat.** This is a simple game or exercise that you can do at any team meeting. One person is on "the hot seat" and everyone else takes turns offering praise, appreciation, and gratitude for that person's contributions to the team and organization. Take turns. You can do one person per meeting to make it last for weeks. Then rinse and repeat.

"Appreciation is about people and their value," says Mike Robbins, author of *Bring Your Whole Self to Work,* where he writes about this exercise. "You create an environment where people feel valued and appreciated for who they are, not just what they do."

Robbins says people start off hesitantly when playing "Appreciation Hot Seat," feeling awkward and a bit vulnerable. But the experience often ends in laughter and hugs—not because they're praising successful business deals or admirable reports, but because they're getting at something deeper.

- **Create a gratitude wall. Or website. Or…**There are many examples of this, in many forms. It's like having a public suggestion box, but instead of suggestions, the notes are expressions of gratitude and appreciation. It can be a bulletin board in the break room with note cards. Or a Slack channel. Keep it simple and make it easy to contribute. (I've seen elaborate versions of this, powered by expensive, proprietary software platforms, too.) Even if you are not in charge of these kinds of things where you work, let's hope that those who are will support the idea and help launch it!

- **Start a gratitude journal.** An abundance of research has found this to be one of the best things you can do to change your life. Really. If you need a place to start, try *The Gratitude Project: How the Science of Thankfulness Can Rewire Our Brains for Resilience, Optimism, and the Greater Good.* There's truly no right or wrong way to do this, as long as you do something. I use a little book called *The 5-Minute Journal,* which prompts me to write three things that I'm thankful for each day, but all you really need is a 99-cent spiral notebook and a pen. It's that easy.

To level-up your gratitude, write thank-you notes or an occasional gratitude letter to someone. T'wina Nobles sends weekly handwritten correspondence to family, friends, community members, and others. "I have tons of stationery, and I have always made it a point to slow down and say thank you to those around me," T'wina says. "I even mail notes or letters to the kids and my husband. In fact, I mail letters to my husband almost monthly and have since we started dating."

Near the end of 2020, I asked T'wina what she was feeling grateful for. "I'm grateful for employment, housing, food, transportation, and the stability I've been able to provide our family."

T'wina then made a good point to end this chapter: don't forget to thank yourself, too.

PART 3

WELCOME TO THE FUTURE

CHAPTER 19

NEVER WASTE A GOOD CRISIS

"We sat down and said there's no other option, we're not going to let this fail."

—BRAD BENSON

Lynn Edwards has spent the last three decades planning and executing events of all kinds, all over the world. Live events, with hundreds or thousands of people, caterers, bartenders, vendor booths, and all the other trappings of work-related conferences. Microsoft and Amazon are among the companies that have hired her services over the years, and for good reason: she's a bundle of cheerful energy, relentlessly creative, and a master problem-solver. And if you know anything about event planning, you know it's usually a matter of solving one problem after another.

"As planners, we are creative and resourceful," Lynn says.[135] "If we were doing an event and ran out of shrimp, I'd ask, 'what else you got back there?' Just give me a problem you think I can't solve."

I've seen Lynn's problem-solving superpowers first-hand. In 2014, I hired her to help me stage a grilled cheese sandwich competition we named The Big Melt. The goal of the event was to promote an iPhone app for food photography, called Fork, that I'd helped build. I was trying to grow awareness for the app and the brand at the time, and what better way to positively influence potential users than melted cheese?

We created the event from scratch, and were struggling to sell tickets. We had to inform the competing vendors in advance of how many sandwiches to be prepared to make, so we made our best guess. On a sunny September day in Seattle, we ended up turning people away at the door after a couple hours, because the maximum number of 400 people had already come through. All the vendors ran out of sandwich materials, but Lynn worked her magic to make sure everyone found their way to the ice cream truck and beer garden. Everyone went home happy—especially the folks from Watershed Pub & Kitchen, who received the most votes for best grilled cheese sandwich.

The year 2020 gave Lynn a massive problem to solve, of course. In March, Lynn and her small team found themselves alone in a massive hotel, facing a new challenge for the first time: how do you stage a live event just days after executive orders to "stay safe at home" would keep more than 1,000 people who had purchased tickets from actually attending in person? As the year progressed, virtual events were to become commonplace, but in early March the idea was still unproven. "Had someone said you have to take the whole thing online, I would have said that's crazy," Lynn remembers thinking. "Now people say, weren't there virtual events before? No, there weren't."

The bigger the change, the bigger the opportunity. Lynn rallied her small team and worked with the event's sponsors to retool the entire plan and move it online. They discounted the price of the ticket to attend, and moved forward. Over three days, there were twenty-four sessions with sixty speakers and forty "booths" for sponsors. Not to mention a shiny new business model for Lynn and her team.

"After it ended, my team and I popped a bottle of champagne and sat there looking at one another. We were the only ones in this massive empty hotel ballroom, and it was like, 'what the hell did we just do?'" says Lynn.

Lynn Edwards

As the pandemic forced stay-at-home orders and travel restrictions across the nation and around the world, all live events were cancelled—and with them, all of Lynn's business. Leveraging their new experience, Lynn and her team quickly pivoted into the business of virtual events, learning everything they could as fast as possible. "It was a Herculean mental lift," Lynn told me. "When everything fell off the books, I took everything under the sun."

Lynn even started doing some basic computer coding—something she'd never done in thirty years of event planning—so she could help customize one of the online platforms. It was just one of many firsts for her and her team. By the end of 2020, they had hosted fifty virtual events, six of them in one week, using fifteen different online platforms. It turned out to be the best year ever for Lynn's business, thanks in part to lower overhead costs and no travel, even though her team would normally do twice as many events in previous years.

By the end of 2020, Lynn would be speaking at an event herself—to 150 other event planners, educating them on how to successfully execute events in a virtual world.

"I created a whole new business," says Lynn, who also appeared in a *Wired* magazine article on virtual events in December of that year. "Here I was, a subject matter expert with thirty years of experience doing one thing, and now I'm doing a 'how-to' university of everything I'd ever learned. I'm thinking: 'Who's life is this?'"

In-person gatherings will resume eventually, but innovations born during the pandemic will remain, according to that *Wired* article.[136] This prediction could be applicable to most—maybe all—industries that survived the pandemic of 2020. Forced innovation in the face of massive disruption led many people to resurface a saying that has been around for decades: "Don't waste a good crisis."

Originally appearing in medical circles, "Don't Waste a Crisis—Your Patient's or Your Own" is the title of a 1976 article by M. F. Weiner in the journal *Medical Economics*.[137] While Weiner meant that a medical crisis can be used to improve aspects of personality, mental health, or lifestyle, the same can be applied to your life at work, at home, and throughout your world.

"When written in Chinese, the word 'crisis' is composed of two characters," John F. Kennedy once said. "One represents danger and the other represents opportunity."[138]

 **BUTTERFLY IMPACT SIGNPOST**

A crisis forces us to think differently. It also forces us to act differently. Those actions can temporarily salve a situation that feels like an emergency, or they can be the foundation for transformation. The latter requires that individuals seize opportunities that probably didn't exist before, much as Lynn and her team did in pulling off dozens of virtual events after doing one for the first time.

"In a crisis, don't hide behind anything or anybody," said Bear Bryant, the legendary Alabama football coach.[139] "They're going to find you anyway."

The year 2020 will be remembered by many as one crisis after another. The global pandemic had countless negative impacts. Nevertheless, it triggered the transformation and growth that individuals and organizations created, conjured, and summoned while navigating new obstacles and challenges.

It also necessitated a change in the way life would be lived going forward. The bigger the change, the bigger the opportunity.

BURNING THE BOATS

Brad Benson opened Stoup Brewing in 2013 with his wife, Lara Zahaba, and a third partner, Robyn Schumacher. Brad and I grew up together, were roommates in college, started our lives together in Seattle after graduation, and served as the best man in each other's weddings. I have supported the brewery from the beginning. *I know, tough duty, but what are friends for?* When Brad made the decision to quit his job as an environmental chemist for more than twenty years, we talked about "burning the boats" and how there would be no turning back; it had to work.

I built Stoup's first website, and have tried to help Brad think through business strategy as the company expanded over the years. In 2019, Stoup added an extra 6,000 square feet of production space in a new building behind the existing beer garden, giving Brad the ability to triple Stoup's beer production. Then the pandemic hit in early 2020, and the more than one-hundred bars and restaurants around Seattle that had been pouring Stoup stopped serving anything to anyone, and shuttered their doors to help slow the spread of the virus. At the time Stoup rarely put its beer in cans or other packages; it made almost all of its money from draft beer, poured into glasses and consumed at bars and restaurants, or in the tap-room at the brewery.

Fortunately for Brad and Stoup, he had already scheduled a special brew to be put into cans the week of the lockdown, using a mobile canning operation. These operations served small breweries that couldn't afford the expense, or have the space, for a permanent canning line. When the shutdown cut off almost all of Stoup's revenue, Brad saw an opportunity.

"We had the canning company scheduled months before and would have done one-hundred cases," Brad says.[140] "After the shutdown I called and asked, Can we do one-thousand?"

Brad Benson

Even though the canning company couldn't accommodate such a short-notice request (and the most it could do in a single day is 600), the craft brewing community is incredibly supportive of one another. What many would see as the competition, local brewers see as members of the same team. Brad says brewers in Seattle were constantly on the phone with one another, sharing ideas and solving problems together. Several breweries had purchased single-serve canning machines in recent years that sat on the back of the bar and were meant to fill a handful of thirty-two-ounce cans per day. When that became the only way to sell beer—and make money—breweries wore them out, filling 300 cans per day.

"The brewing community really came together, and we were all calling each other," Brad says. "Who's got cans? Who's got lids? Everyone just helping each other out."

One of those brewer friends eventually tipped Brad off that a much bigger brewery in town, Elysian, had purchased a new, large-scale canning line and would be looking to sell its old machine. Breweries around the nation were looking to make the same pivot to cans that Stoup was eyeing, so the market for canning equipment was rapidly becoming incredibly tight.

Brad called and negotiated a fast sale, and by June Stoup had its own permanent canning line up and running. It was a big expense to take on at a time when the brewery's revenue had almost entirely disappeared, but Brad felt the risk needed to be taken.

Before the pandemic, 99 percent of Stoup's revenue that didn't come from the taproom at the brewery was generated by draft, poured at restaurants and bars around the city. By the end of 2020, 75 percent of revenue came from packaged beer, sold in cans in grocery stores and specialty beer markets. Stoup brought in more revenue in December of 2020 than it had in December of 2019 (even though the profit margin was much lower).

It was still a rough year for Stoup, and for so many other small businesses. Brad and his founding partners took a pay cut to help avoid any layoffs, and Brad spent countless hours filling out paperwork for government aid and other programs designed to help businesses impacted by the pandemic. But Stoup ended the year on a positive note, with more staff than before the pandemic because of the shift in the business model, and the experience and learning from having gone through some of the darkest days a small business can face.

"I came back to those initial conversations of 'burning the boats,'" Brad says. "We sat down and said there's no other option, we're not going to let this fail. What can we do today to move this forward?"

∗ ∗ ∗

Change is inevitable, but progress is optional (Chapter 3). Personal progress came in many shapes and sizes in 2020, all driven by a handful of truths that would have surprised us at the beginning of the year.

We are resilient—and adaptable. According to one Pew study, around four in ten US adults said in August 2020 that they, or someone in their household, had been laid off, lost their job, or taken a pay cut.[141] The same study found that a substantial majority of US adults (86 percent) said that there is some kind of lesson, or set of lessons, for mankind to learn from the coronavirus outbreak.

We turned to baking, gardening, board games, nature walks, and bird watching. And got serious about washing our hands. At the beginning of the pandemic, an emphasis on hand washing, including singing "Happy Birthday" to ensure twenty seconds of cleaning, produced countless memes and conversations, not to mention a significant improvement in personal hygiene.

We staged drive-by graduation parades, driveway birthday parties, and Thanksgiving tailgating dinners. We opened gifts on Christmas over Zoom. We adapted to wearing masks, working out at home, and picking up takeout from local restaurants to help support them. *While giving us a reason to leave the house.*

We found new value in family, relationships, and dinner. Nearly 70 percent of people in the Pew study said that they were more appreciative of family and friends as a result of the year's challenges.

For the first time since at least the Great Depression, a majority of young adults in the US were living with their parents in 2020. Many of those families were eating together, too. This is a marked change: before the pandemic, only 30 percent to 40 percent of families typically shared a meal together, according to research done by Anne Fishel, an associate clinical professor of psychology at Harvard University and co-founder of the Family Dinner Project. "Seventy percent of families are cooking more, 60 percent of families are making meals from scratch, 50 percent of them are involving kids, and there are 55 percent more family meals overall," she says, citing research done by Canada's Guelph University.[142]

We moved online. Much as Lynn Edwards discovered in moving an events business online, friends and family turned to virtual meetings on holidays, and for weekly trivia nights and happy hour gatherings. Few people I know had ever done a family video call before 2020. I can't think of anyone who hasn't done one after 2020. The awkwardness of being on camera in our homes eventually dissipated, both for work calls and catching up with family. By the end of the year, it felt normal to "jump on a Zoom" with parents, friends, or a community group. Musical artists, symphonies, personal trainers, yoga instructors, city councils, and religious gatherings all found their audiences and communities online. How many years would that have taken without the pandemic?

We slowed down and reflected. The cult of busy disappeared, at least outside of work. Weekends and evenings suddenly opened up. I canceled seven trips, four for work and three personal, in March 2020. Traffic eased up in cities when people were forced to stop commuting. A popular meme on social media during the start of the crisis reflected this: "It's like the Earth told everyone to go to their room and think about what they had done." The environment emerged as one of the beneficiaries of the crisis, at least in the beginning. Traffic in cities and in the skies ground to a halt, giving air quality a desperately needed…breather.

People got a breather, too. The concept of FOMO (Fear of Missing Out) disappeared overnight since there was nothing to miss out on anymore. We took advantage of the chance to reflect on all those activities, events, and other busyness we had built our lives around. Some we missed desperately. Others we found a way to live without. And maybe found a better use for our time instead.

We became activists. Following the police killings of Ahmaud Arbery in February, Breonna Taylor in March, and George Floyd in May, millions of people around the nation and around the world took to the streets to make their protest voices heard in the name of Black Lives Matter (BLM). Somewhere between 15 million and 26 million people in the US articipated in demonstrations by the end of June, according to polls and research cited by *The New York Times*.[143] "These figures would make the recent protests the largest movement in the country's history, according to interviews with scholars and crowd-counting experts," the *Times* reported in July 2020. And the demonstrations continued throughout the year.

While the biggest cities received the most media coverage, there were events in towns, neighborhoods, and communities of all sizes. I marched with about 3,000 others in one peaceful event in Tacoma, Washington. Between May 24 and August 22, there were more than 10,600 BLM protest events in the US, according to research by Armed Conflict Location & Event Data Project (ACLED).[144] The same research found that 93 percent of protests were peaceful, with no reports of violence or vandalism.

And we voted. That passion became action when more votes were cast in the 2020 presidential election than in any other US election in history. The turnout rate of registered voters was the highest in more than a century, too.[145]

We built resilience. We flexed new muscles of adaptability. We paused, and reflected, and valued our lives differently. Above all, we can hope that we learned lessons that will power us in 2021 and beyond.

"It was such an accelerator," Lynn says, reflecting on 2020. "There's probably some stuff we should have been doing all along, of course. But it required us as business owners to find a different way. At the end of the day, I'm in the gathering business. That's what I do for a living."

Admittedly, she and her team finished the year exhausted by finding new ways of doing things all year. Who didn't? Resilience is developed through facing adversity—like the time the online platform Lynn was using crashed one hour into an event with 500 people logged in. Lynn received eighty-seven text messages in about thirty seconds, she told me, then simply turned her phone off. She said it's the first time she had ever "just shut down," while adding that she went on to reschedule the event, which then went ahead as planned.

"I've never been in a hotel that burned down the day of an event," Lynn says with a chuckle. "I've had some fetal-position, crying moments. But I'm always looking at the positive. I mean, I had good stories before, but 2020…"

It will certainly be a year that stands out for anyone who went through it. Let's take those lessons learned and turn them into lasting change, for the better.

MAKING IT HAPPEN

Take some time, today or tomorrow, to stop and reflect on what you personally overcame, or learned, or changed in 2020 that you carried forward into your life today—or wish you had carried forward. Write it down. Then ask someone in your life what they learned in 2020. The shared experience of finding silver linings is a powerful way to acknowledge them and keep them alive.

Your brain changed in 2020. It processed things you probably never imagined or thought possible before the pandemic. You can benefit from those changes, from that *neuroplasticity.*

"When our brain changes, we change," James Doty wrote in *Into the Magic Shop.*[146] "That is a truth proven by science. But an even greater truth is that when our heart changes, everything changes. And that change is not only in how we see the world but in how the world sees us. And in how the world responds to us."

CHAPTER 20

———

WORK. LIFE. BLENDED.

"Where you spend your time is what you value."
—GIANNA BISCONTINI

Joe Hurd is an investor, advisor, and mentor to startup technology companies in San Francisco and around the Bay Area. When COVID-19 shut down life in March 2020, he seized the opportunity to work on himself. He stopped drinking alcohol, prioritized at least seven hours of sleep each night, and replaced commuting two hours in his car with 12,000 steps each day.

"It feels pretty selfish, more of just for me, looking inward," says Joe, who shed thirty pounds between March and December.[147] "That radiated out and manifested itself in so many positive ways, from me not snapping at my family when I got home from work, or being able to take on more projects because I didn't have that second glass of wine at 9 p.m."

Joe Hurd

Joe's story exemplifies the power of pulling small levers to make positive changes in the world around you, which is the premise of this book. None of it would have been possible without the pandemic causing shelter-in-place orders that disrupted his usually busy work life. He seized the opportunity. He didn't waste the crisis.

"I turned inward and said to myself, 'I want one thing to look back on that I accomplished [during the pandemic],'" Joe says. "I feel selfish; it's not something I did for society as a whole, or for my company. But getting my personal health in control and taking ownership over my weight, my eating, my drinking: those were making the biggest impact in my work life and then my home life."

Joe learned an important lesson of how The Butterfly Impact can cause a ripple effect throughout his life and his world. By focusing on his personal health and well-being—which felt selfish to him—he improved his ability to show up in the other parts of his life, the parts that don't feel selfish.

"It's all part of one continuous circle," Joe says. "I've become much more productive in my work. I'm operating at my peak. In doing so, I'm a happier person, a better employee, and better at home. I am the sum total of those individual parts."

BUTTERFLY IMPACT SIGNPOST

Before 2020, people strived to find work-life balance. Once the pandemic hit, most were faced with work-life blending, especially if they were suddenly working from home for the first time. Work meetings, deadlines, and deliverables intermixed with home chores, mealtime, maybe helping the kids, and finding your own space. Meanwhile, those who lived alone faced a different challenge: isolation. Millions of people were cut off from the social outlet of the office almost overnight.

The pandemic erased the physical, geographical, and psychological dividers between our work lives and our personal lives. Instead of separate experiences, they became one. The melding of these two worlds forced new challenges—and new opportunities.

"Why was I running so hard? Where'd all that time go?" asked Rob Acker, a college friend who runs Salesforce.org, a nonprofit philanthropy.[148] "Never before have you had to be more of a self-starter. Society was always plugging you into one event or another and we would look forward to those events. Now you're 100 percent reliant on you for your happiness."

Time saved from a commute or a work trip became time for something else. Deciding how to spend that time was a new test for many. Some quickly filled up the time with more work, which was understandable, given how many companies and industries were rocked by the pandemic. That sense of urgency was difficult to control. Others, especially parents, had their non-work time filled up with helping their kids navigate online school or, like me, tutoring algebra. Turning inward like Joe did, however, was the best recipe for growth and managing the crisis.

Use extra time to focus on your own health and well-being. The need for extra effort and attention to our own well-being extended beyond capitalizing on a few additional hours each week, thanks to working remotely. The psychological and emotional toll of 2020 hit many people hard with its unrelenting negative news cycle; "doomscrolling" emerged as a new mental health problem. Consuming large quantities of negative news online can be harmful. You don't need a professional to tell you that. Anyone who fell into a rabbit hole of reading news about the spreading of COVID-19 and the deaths it caused, social injustices, and the bitter partisan politics and conspiracy theories swirling around the US presidential election was at risk of coming out of the year feeling worse, not better.

Yet another reason to focus on health and well-being in the face of adversity and uncertainty.

Take care of yourself first. The fact that Joe felt selfish for his focus on his own health is not surprising. As I mentioned in Part 1, self-help is selfish—in a good way, but one that runs counter to most of our culture. We're raised to believe that giving of ourselves is the ultimate goal, at the expense of investing in ourselves. The opposite is actually true: "None of the other stuff is going to work if the animal that you live in is just a broke-down mess," author Elizabeth Gilbert once said.[149]

Think of the instruction on a pre-flight safety briefing: in the unlikely event the cabin loses oxygen, put your mask on first. You're no good to the rest of your family if you can't breathe yourself.

I spoke with dozens of people in 2020 who had discovered a new drive to take care of themselves first. In most cases, the extra time forced upon us by the pandemic created an opportunity that many, like Joe, had been struggling to create before COVID-19. That so many of us turned to health and practices to support well-being will long be remembered as one of the silver linings of the pandemic. We can hope that most of us will carry these practices forward and sustain this change in our lives even after the pandemic subsides, and life returns to a sense of normality.

"Where you spend your time is what you value." Blending work and life together gave us an opportunity, maybe for the first time, to actually prioritize our personal needs and values. Gone were the barriers holding us back from what we always thought we'd pursue. It turned out to be a good test, too, of what we actually valued, as opposed to what we assumed or hoped we valued.

"Where you spend your time is what you value," says Gianna Biscontini, an executive leadership and well-being coach and author who has worked with a number of A-list business leaders.[150] "Values are usually aspirational; we need to hold them up to our actions as a test."

Gianna Biscontini

Gianna explains that this is like looking at a transparent sheet like the kind that teachers would use with old-school overhead projectors; one layer would have the printed math problem, for example, and then the next layer would have the written solution. Imagine the printed layer listing your stated values, and the transparent overhead listing how you actually spend your time. Would they match up?

Before the pandemic, it was easy to say, "if only I didn't have that work trip, or the weekend soccer tournament," I would prioritize that thing I've always said I value. After work and life blended together, we had more control over matching our values with how we spent our time. According to the research, that autonomy is essential to our psychological and physiological well-being.

"We had so much going for us and we didn't even know it," Gianna told me. "Lack of autonomy can take down your mental and physical health quicker than almost anything. We're humans; we're meant to be free and to have free choices."

Her advice: run experiments to increase your well-being, understand what you need, and—most of all—"be unapologetic" about it.

"How valuable are you to me when you're cranky, and your relationship is suffering, and you're not sleeping?" she says. "Your brain is cloudy, you're not showing up in meetings like I need you to, your focus is gone, right? We're humans, we're not machines."

"HOW VALUABLE ARE YOU TO ME WHEN YOU'RE CRANKY, AND YOUR RELATIONSHIP IS SUFFERING, AND YOU'RE NOT SLEEPING?"

Gianna says her "shining-light memory" from 2020 will be that the year gave us permission to do what we needed to do anyway. Because we weren't getting that permission from anything else.

To implement Gianna's advice, use your calendar to prioritize well-being. Ever heard the financial advice to "pay yourself first"? It's the same approach here. Start small, and schedule short blocks of time for disconnection from email, a quick walk, or social time with family.

Look at your calendar for next week: do you see your values anywhere on there? Be "unapologetic" about what you need. Unless it's on your calendar, it probably won't happen.

Set and practice clear boundaries. The blending of work with life made setting boundaries essential to personal happiness and well-being. The gravitational pull of Zoom calls and emails, once they invaded our living rooms and kitchens, quickly became difficult to resist. Back-to-back-to-back video calls that filled out a full day on a calendar made people feel even more busy working from home than they ever had when they were going into the office. And, given the surrounding stress of the pandemic and everything else that happened in 2020, stress and burnout emerged as larger problems for employers and employees to directly address than ever before.

The stress, fear, and anxiety that stretched throughout 2020 put extreme pressure on our finite mental, emotional, and physical resources. Psychologists call this allostatic overload, which refers to the cost of chronic or extreme wear and tear on our bodies, minds, and emotions. Allostatic overload occurs when we run out of capacity to manage these negative effects.

Many information workers, used to spending the day at the computer, also dealt with cognitive overload. Navigating remote communication tools and reinventing one's job on the fly while working from home exceeded the brain's ability to keep track of everything going on. It was like having a computer with too many software programs and browser tabs open at once: the CPU spins faster and faster, the internal fan clicks on to help cool the system, but the laptop is suddenly too hot to sit on your lap. It needs a break. Throughout much of 2020, so did our brains and emotions.

Clear boundaries between work and life emerged as an essential element in managing the overwhelm and uncertainty in 2020.

- **Be intentional about breaks.** Set a calendar invitation and block out the time for a break. Even short breaks can make a big impact; anything that puts you in a positive mental space for five, ten, fifteen, or thirty minutes is a great place to start. You might also try the 20-20-20 rule if you spend all day staring at a computer screen: Every twenty minutes, pause and look at something twenty feet away for twenty seconds. Research found this to be helpful in preventing eye strain; try it as a way to reduce psychological pressure.

- **Move your body.** Any form of aerobic exercise, including walking, reduces stress hormones such as adrenaline and cortisol, and stimulates the production of endorphins, the neurochemicals in the brain that are natural mood elevators. Even five minutes of stretching or sit-ups or jumping jacks lower stress and lift your mood. Schedule it into your calendar. If possible, and make it the same time every day so you can be consistent.

- **Experiment with disrupting workplace inertia.** Imagine that you've just started your job and have a blank slate. Limit your meetings to forty-five and twenty-five minutes, instead of the customary sixty and thirty. Block off two hours each day—every day—when you don't take meetings or answer email and instead do deep-focus work, or just spend time thinking. Establish a start time and end time for your day and communicate that to your team. And no emails or calls on nights and weekends.

  If this sounds extreme and not plausible where you work, try it as a two-week experiment. Tell your boss you want to "see what happens" and then reevaluate. You may not keep all the changes, but even if you only keep one or two, that's progress.

- **Establish routines and schedules.** You learned about values, systems, and making lists in earlier chapters. The combination of life in lockdown, working from home, and perhaps having children and family right there next to you, requires us to embrace those tools. Develop them and adapt your daily schedule to prioritize them. If quality time with family is something you value, set a time each day or each week to make sure it happens. When you make sure that you have the time, what you actually do with it will take care of itself. I played Mario Kart with my boys many nights when I couldn't interest them in a movie or documentary. They enjoy beating Dad in video games whenever they can, and I've found that when my kids are happy, everything is better.

I know people who set a calendar reminder to go for a walk at 5 p.m. every day. I know others who begin the day with a longer-than-usual walk with their dog. Without travel, scheduled events, or other calendar-driven predictability, we learned to fill in the uncanny free-floating hours with activities that helped us cope and gave us a little life. At least we tried.

"As obnoxious as I find schedules and routines, these saved my ass this year," author Mark Manson wrote in a post on his website Life Lessons from 2020.[151] "And as horrified as I am by my newfound predictability, I will probably be keeping many of these routines post-pandemic."

MORE TIME AT HOME

Bill Gates predicts that more than half of business travel is not coming back.[152] For those of us whose jobs previously required multiple trips per month, this would be good for our health: One Harvard study found that business travelers who spent fourteen or more nights away from home per month had significantly higher body mass index scores and were notably more likely to report poorer scores in areas such as anxiety, depression, alcohol dependence, and sleep than those of individuals who traveled for six days or less per month.

"What definitely goes is flying cross-country for a four-hour business meeting," Joe Hurd said, when asked what is not coming back after the pandemic, jokingly referring to this as "show up and throw up." Joe admits that he will only "stay off the plane as long as my competitors do" but is hopeful that people will be much more judicious when deciding on work travel.

In addition to less travel, many workplace experts predict some combination of a hybrid work model will emerge in the years following the pandemic. In industries that can accommodate it, workers will likely adopt a schedule of working two to three days a week in the office while working from home the rest. This makes learning from our experiences of dealing with the pandemic—spending time on health and well-being, setting clear boundaries, and showing up as our whole selves at work and home—even more important.

"We have a stress response in our bodies that, back in the cave-woman days, it's like 'Oh, there's a tiger' or 'there's a rustling bush and my life is in danger,'" Gianna says. "There is no biological mechanism for hope. And so, we have to create our own. Creating hope in our lives is what I hope people take out of 2020. You can consciously endeavor to create your own mechanism for hope and positivity and improvement. And well-being is definitely included in all of that."

MAKING IT HAPPEN

As we put the pieces back together from the massive disruption caused by the pandemic, be "unapologetic" about prioritizing well-being in your life. It is the big rock that all the other little rocks need to fall around.

CHAPTER 21

THE NEW WAY TO WORK

"I'd consider my life well-lived if I took time to eat lunch during the workday almost every day."

—RUCHIKA TULSHYAN

How did you learn to make friends? It's one of the most important parts of life; research has found over and over that people at the end of their lives rank relationships as the leading measure of happiness, and of feeling they lived a fulfilled life. Yet it's mostly left to chance in our culture.

I consider myself one of the luckier people on the planet in this regard, and my fortune came early in life. I had a great group of friends in sixth grade (whom I'm still in contact with today), but the following year we were heading to one of two junior high schools in town, and I lived on the wrong side of the boundary—by one block. That meant my friends were going to one school and I would attend the other. My mom asked the school district for a waiver, but was told No. So, I showed up in seventh grade frustrated, stressed, anxious, and mostly determined to hate my new school. All students were given a class schedule generated by a computer, and as the day went on, I ended up with the same person in nearly every class: Brad Benson, the brewery founder you met in Chapter 20. The computer had assigned us to the same six classes and, thanks to our surnames both starting with the same letter, we sat alongside one another in most of them.

The butterfly effect of this seemingly small change in my life—my class schedule in seventh grade—had a greater impact on both of us than can accurately be measured. Nearly forty years later we remain close friends. We were roommates in college and as we started our lives after graduation. We were the best man in each other's wedding. Our parents even have places on our hometown Idaho lake near one another so we can reunite each summer.

Lucky, right? Yet I've never worked with Brad, outside of building him a barebones website and helping him clean up the brewery at closing time a handful of times when they first opened up. Like you, I don't spend nearly as much time with my personal friends as I do talking to people I work with. Developing healthy workplace relationships was hard enough before the pandemic changed the way many of us work. With more remote work, less commuting, and less work travel, how will we foster friendships at work?

Shasta Nelson knows how. She is a friendship expert, and has written three books on the topic after realizing more than a decade ago that people needed help in this area. She helps clients as an organizational consultant, and points to research that continues to reveal the majority of people are struggling to forge friendships deeper than a dinner plate.

Shasta Nelson

"I started looking for friendship resources for (my clients)," Shasta said, when she told me about how she got started years ago.[153] "They could go online to find a marriage, a job, a house, every life goal they have. But there was hardly anything about building friendships as an adult. I started asking, 'Why is nobody talking about this?' We are obsessed with the parent-child relationship and romantic relationships, when those are really the fewer relationships we will have in our life." Having friends is a significant factor to living a fulfilled and meaningful life.

In her latest book, *The Business of Friendship: Making the Most of Our Relationships Where We Spend Most of Our Time*, Shasta takes everything she's learned in researching and coaching and presents it through the lens of the workplace. Research has long shown that employees who have a best friend at work are more engaged, less likely to leave, have fewer accidents, call out sick less, and feel prouder of their employer. Our work is the place where adults most commonly find friends.

"It's been great to see the recognition of how loneliness is permeating our lives. [Friendship]'s not just the fluffy, nice-to-have thing," Shasta says. "It's the number-one thing for our happiness, by far. It's the biggest influence on our health besides maybe sleep. It's big."

 BUTTERFLY IMPACT SIGNPOST

While the suddenly new world of work has required us to learn the skills of video calls and advanced digital communication, relationships and collaboration still matter most. Through the process of researching and writing this book, I found over and over again that the key to unlocking fulfillment at work is all the relationships and basic human interaction. I didn't know that would be the outcome when I started this project, but it became crystal clear to me as the writer about halfway through the process. I hope that it's become clear to you as the reader, too.

In 2020, relationships at work gained attention that had been previously lacking. When millions of people were abruptly forced to work from home, the spontaneous conversations at the coffee station and in the conference room vanished. We had to start thinking intentionally in new ways about personal connections and relationships with co-workers. It was a step in the right direction. Thinking of friendship and personal interaction as a skill may be new for many people. Making friends and talking to people is an ability we're just born with, right? Wrong.

"We're scared of not knowing how to interact with people, we're scared of the things that could go wrong with human interactions," Shasta says. "We are scared of confrontation, we're scared of having hard conversations honestly."

Shasta reports that we replace half our close friends roughly every seven years, so we should get plenty of practice. Drawing on extensive social science research, she identified three nonnegotiable requirements of a relationship and used them to build the Frientimacy Triangle. Like a mathematic equation, a healthy relationship must practice all three: positivity (positive emotions), consistency (reliable interactions and shared experiences), and vulnerability (mutual sharing).

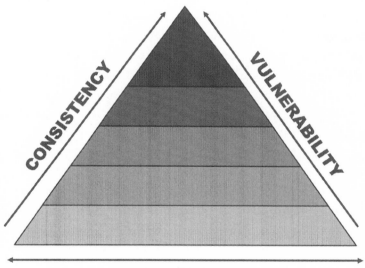

Healthy relationships start with positivity at the bottom of the Triangle, and develop in an escalating and incremental way up both sides of the Triangle. "If positivity isn't built on, the other two are almost impossible to achieve," Shasta says.

We can evaluate the health of any corporate culture, any team, and any relationship based on how they practice these three things. During Shasta's assessments of teams at various companies, she says, most people have expected the vulnerability score to be the lowest, but around 80 percent of teams score the lowest in positivity. And finding positivity in 2020 was even more challenging, of course.

"The dearth of positive emotions (at work)—it's so sad," Shasta says. "In my opinion, it's one of the easiest ones to actually lift up."

In a world of remote work, it's even more important. Shasta defines positivity as the desire to leave people feeling something positive, and it is something we can give to everyone. You don't have to be a manager, or the leader of the video call or meeting. Every interaction is a chance to spread more positivity around your world. For starters:

- **Show warmth.** Eye contact and a smile can make a big impact on others.

- **Show appreciation.** Thank a colleague for helping with a project, or offer a compliment for something. (This is even more important when you're feeling stressed or distracted.)

- **Show empathy.** If someone shares good news, cheer them on. If they share frustrations, groan with them a little.

Shasta says that appreciation and validation are what are most missing in the workplace. And everyone has the ability to make a difference. In our new era of remote working, doing this has become even more vital.

OFFICE WORK WITHOUT OFFICES

In 2005, Matt Mullenweg invited a couple volunteer programmers to join a new company he wanted to create. They said Yes, and a company named Automattic was born to support the open-source WordPress web publishing platform. The software they created is now used by more than 60 million websites, including almost 40 percent of the top 10 million websites as of January 2021. The company had more than 1,200 employees in September 2020, but no central office. Everyone works remotely, and always has.

When millions of people joined them in 2020, Mullenweg's company culture and success with managing remote employees became more than a curiosity. What had Automattic learned in fifteen years of distributed work that the rest of the world can learn from?

In 2013, my friend Scott Berkun (whom you met in Chapter 1) spent a year working for Automattic under a special arrangement through which he would also be writing a book about working there. *A Year Without Pants: WordPress.com and the Future of Work* is a collection of his insights and experiences.[154] I asked him what lesson from Automattic's experience he would most recommend to organizations forced into the massive shift to remote work in 2020. While he often mentioned platforms and tools such as Zoom, Slack, and Microsoft Teams, his chief insight was one step removed from the tools.

"When it comes to Automattic, they're just better communicators, and it improves their ability to use any of these tools well," Scott told me. "People who work there write well. It seems obvious and stupid, and you're probably thinking 'doesn't everybody write well?' No, they don't!"

Scott says that, in most organizations, there's a lot of terrible communication. People are unable to be concise, for example, or ask clarifying questions—all these little but essential habits that we take for granted.

The bigger problem is that leaders are often the worst communicators.

"They don't read email, or they read the first paragraph and they assume a lot, or they ramble," Scott says. "Leaders can say all kinds of stuff about what's important or not, but what defines culture and how people behave is what the leaders actually do. If they're shitty and sloppy and don't read emails and make bad assumptions and just ramble, then they're implying that that's OK, and other people will emulate it."

Many leaders think they're too busy to respond completely, especially to subordinates. But that's bullshit. Chances are that they respond to *their* boss with full sentences, so they *are* able to communicate effectively, if they are willing. Every leader who talks about fostering a healthy culture in which everyone shows respect can take another minute to write a complete sentence in that email reply.

The abilities to communicate clearly and effectively, and to build a healthy, respectful culture with digital communication, are essential to remote work.

After years of leading a distributed organization, Matt Mullenweg identified his Five Levels of Autonomy and the progression of effective distributed work.[155]

Can you imagine doing your job without ever having to attend a meeting? Mullenweg calls that situation Nirvana. It doesn't mean that brainstorming conversations and smaller team huddles don't ever happen, but the traditional staff meeting and status update stand-ups all move to collaborative digital documentation. This is why the ability to write well is so critical to remote work and effective communication: only when you can't rely on written collaboration should you call a meeting.

"I see the bad habits that many managers have," Scott told me. "They've been forced to support remote work, and they've done it. They've been forced to do Zoom calls, maybe they're using Slack or Teams, but they're still trying to replicate what they had, and you can't do that. A lot of traditional managers are simply just scheduling more meetings."

Nobody wants more meetings. Organizations should be leveraging these tools for asynchronous work and allowing people to work on their own time, on their own schedule, because they can still be productive.

"The advantage of working remotely is to allow people to work more independently and rely less on meetings," Scott told me. "It's an easier way to get things done."

Relationships are still important, even in a distributed organization. The Automattic staff spend a few weeks each year meeting in person to develop personal connections. The company has even developed its own software, which assigns seating at meals to connect people from different teams more effectively.

"Any company that can enable their people to be fully effective in a distributed fashion can and should do it [long] after this current crisis has passed," Mullenweg said in March 2020.[156]

"It's a moral imperative. But that doesn't mean it's going to be easy, or that the chaotic and stressful first taste some workplaces are getting right now is one that inspires them to keep trying."

A RECIPE FOR HEALTHY TEAMWORK

One of the consistent traits of high-performing groups, from Navy SEAL teams to agile computer developers, is some version of a regular reflective practice. Matt Thompson, a consultant who works with companies like PepsiCo on team health and collaboration, compares this to a piece of software and the ability for a developer to distribute small improvements as updates.

"It's that ability for a team to get even…one percent happier and more effective together…each week," says Matt, former senior director at the Mozilla Foundation, the non-profit organization with 1,000 volunteer developers contributing to the Firefox web browser.[157] "Teams should have a regular rhythm and ritual for surfacing areas where maybe things aren't going that well, or where people need some extra help, or where it feels like the team is getting stuck."

Some teams call such sessions after-action reviews (or AARs), but only use them following a big project. Companies hire Matt to help them implement his "cookbook" for healthy high-performing teams while he continues to work on his upcoming book, *The Joy of Teamwork*. He calls the reviews "retrospectives" and says it's a known recipe for surfacing what's happening with the team, and then making some small improvements together in a relatively timely, effective, and efficient way. This is applying The Butterfly Impact to your teams. Matt says we should do that all the time, but especially in a post-COVID world.

"The pandemic has had a huge impact on how we're working [and] has had a huge impact on people's mental and emotional and physical health. So, the importance of surfacing these small tensions and challenges and then making improvements, small but steady improvements, together, I think is the most important practice," Matt told me.

WHEN IN DOUBT, EAT LUNCH

"I'd consider my life well lived if I took time to eat lunch during the workday almost every day," says Ruchika Tulshyan, who we met in Chapter 11. "This means not at my desk, not in a meeting or while working, but [while] connecting with someone, or even myself, while I eat mindfully."

This was her approach before the pandemic and, despite all that changed in 2020, Ruchika doubled down and authored an article for the *Harvard Business Review* in 2021 to share with others.[158] Ruchika grew up in Singapore and, because of this, she says she considers lunch "sacred."

Having a "proper, generous lunch break"—especially with co-workers—can help combat burnout and improve collaboration. Research has found that workers who take a lunch break are more satisfied and productive, and report better teamwork when they eat together. You can do this virtually, too, with or without video.

Ruchika says the onus lies on leaders to create the psychological safety for employees to take time for lunch. Managers must ensure that their teams don't get penalized or viewed as less productive, and foster an environment in which taking time for lunch is a norm within the organization. In the 1987 movie *Wall*

Street, Gordon Gekko said, "Lunch is for wimps." That distorted view has unfortunately influenced our unhealthy workplace culture: in research conducted before the pandemic, 62 percent of American workers said they eat lunch at their desks.

"Everyone benefits when workplace lunches are normalized," Ruchika wrote, citing a survey result that North American employees who took a lunch break every day reported higher engagement in their work, based on metrics including job satisfaction, productivity, and likelihood to recommend working there to others.

All of this, of course, falls apart quickly in a culture that still values busyness over controlling one's time. Imagine a video call during which your teammates scoff at your mention of coming back from lunch. "Who has time for lunch? I'm swamped!" I hope we move toward a healthier, more sustainable social construct, beyond the cult of busy, in which someone who takes a lunch break every day is seen as the person who actually has their shit together.

As Gianna Biscontini urged in the previous chapter: "Be unapologetic."

Who is more impressive: the person who is in control of their schedule and their boundaries, or the person who is overwhelmed by their calendar and all the meetings that *other* people are putting there?

"We're so weird as humans," Shasta says. "We don't want to be perceived as being lazy or distracted. We don't know how to interact with most people. Yet we think it would be shameful to have to go and learn that, as if there's something wrong with us."

MAKING IT HAPPEN

There's nothing wrong with us, but we have a new opportunity to make things at work a little better. Hopefully, the ideas in this chapter have given you a place to start.

- **Spread positive energy with your communications.** Make the most of your relationships where you spend the most time.

- **Communicate more clearly.** Write one more sentence, if it will help.

- **Set clear boundaries.** Ask for what you need, and be unapologetic about taking care of you.

- **Make time for lunch.** This seemingly small commitment will make an outsized impact on your day.

CHAPTER 22

LIFE SUCKS. WORK SUCKS. DEAL WITH IT.

"Dude, you are good. You're making plenty of progress."

—DAN HARRIS

If you made it through 2020 without losing your job or getting your pay cut, with your health and the health of your family and loved ones intact, you had a good year. It was easy to be grateful for what you had and appreciate the little things around you, maybe for the first time.

What happens when the pandemic is truly, finally, over? Will we go back to the way things were, and take those things for granted again?

Jennifer Deger, a breast cancer survivor, shares my concern.

"When I was going through treatment, I was ridiculously grate-ful," Jen told me.[159] "[But] it's easy to get wrapped back up in life. I sometimes think, *Wait a minute, you're lucky.* Sometimes I can't believe it happened at all. It's a balance when you're busy and stressed but I don't know how long I get. It does make me think about how hard I'm working, but I really like what I do, and I just want to enjoy it."

Jennifer Deger and Clementine

Jen beat her cancer into remission, and then returned to work at an incredibly stressful job. She is the director of finance—the controller—for the Bill & Melinda Gates Foundation. Jen leads a team of thirty-six people working to distribute more than $6 billion in grants and funding each year. So, when she talks about being stressed at work, it's likely a different stress than you and I feel.

In 2020, Jen helped the Gates Foundation meet the moment in many ways, with her team paying out hundreds of millions of dollars in funding for COVID-related efforts to ensure that lower-income nations had access to vaccines.

"When you're doing it for something so important, it makes a difference. It's amazing to be part of that, but there's just a lot more to do," says Jen, who once bumped into Bono, the U2 lead singer, in the hallway at work. "I'm grateful to have my job, and I think I already had a lot of resilience. [I] just have to keep taking whatever comes. It makes you appreciate your friends and your family, and lets you change all the expectations."

* * *

Our expectations were violated in 2020, says Gianna Biscontini. And when expectations are violated, it's a good time to step back and re-think. The tumult of 2020 compelled us to take stock of what really matters. While it's easy to talk about silver linings in the pandemic, the learnings must endure. If we forget how much change occurred and how much we went through, we will lose the value of the experience.

"I've never had more taken from me," Gianna told me.[160] "I had health issues, business issues, my father passed away, I moved—yet I found myself thinking…I'm so grateful. Not because those things happened—they took me down—but because, when you have so much taken from you, most of us, if we're lucky, become thankful for what's left."

 **BUTTERFLY IMPACT SIGNPOST**

The pandemic—and everything else that happened in 2020—hit everyone hard, at least psychologically and emotionally, if not physically. For many ambitious professionals, it challenged the "power of positive thinking" that many have incorporated as their guiding light to achievement. And yes, I've written extensively on positivity throughout this book, but this final chapter is a heaping dose of sobriety: work-life blending is really hard, and sometimes it just sucks.

During the pandemic, when people were in lockdown, cut off from social life, work, travel, and even their local gym, it became much more difficult to believe that you could dramatically improve your life simply by thinking positive thoughts, creating a vision board, or performing some aspirational goalsetting. The focus for most people quickly became how to mentally manage social isolation, remote work, and, frequently, depression and anxiety.

If you are not inherently a positive thinker—or had thought you were until 2020 hit—consider a different approach: *negative self-help*. The foundation of this approach lies in embracing the cold, hard fact that things often don't work out, happiness isn't easily attainable, and if we lower our expectations enough, happiness will come more easily. Since our expectations were "violated" in 2020, as Gianna said, it seemed like a good time to give it a shot.

I first encountered this approach through a book called *The Antidote: Happiness for People Who Can't Stand Positive Thinking* by Oliver Burkeman.[161] As you know by now, I've devoured and celebrated more than my fair share of positive-thinking books, articles, frameworks, and yes, inspirational quotes. Just ask my teenage sons. *Or picture their tandem eye roll.*

Burkeman spent several years reporting on the field of psychology as a journalist and writes that he came to a "startling conclusion" about what united all the psychologists and philosophers he had interviewed and researched over his career.

"The startling conclusion at which they had all arrived, in different ways, was this: that the effort to try to feel happy is often precisely the thing that makes us miserable," Burkeman writes. "And that it is our constant efforts to eliminate the negative— insecurity, uncertainty, failure, or sadness—that is what causes us to feel insecure, anxious, uncertain, or unhappy."

This approach isn't new. Aspects of it have been around for generations, from Stoicism to Buddhism. Burkeman winds together a delightful collection of counterpoint wisdom based on "learning to enjoy uncertainty, embracing insecurity, stopping trying to think positively, becoming familiar with failure, even learning to value death."

Learning to value death notwithstanding, the other attributes of negative self-help seem to fit perfectly into a pandemic world. Uncertainty and insecurity ruled for months, and there was no running away from them—or outthinking them with a pithy quote or daily affirmation. As the 2015 Pixar movie *Inside Out* taught us, there is no joy without sadness. And as the growing awareness of *toxic positivity* reinforces,[162] the overgeneralization of a happy, optimistic state may result in the denial, minimization, and invalidation of the authentic human experience.

IT COULD BE WORSE: NEGATIVE VISUALIZATION

Mark Manson, author of *The Subtle Art of Not Giving a F*uck* and *Everything is F*cked: A Book About Hope*, is another proponent of negative self-help. "When I wrote my books, I wrote them with this approach in mind. Life sucks. Deal with it,"

Manson wrote in an article called "6 Books That Will Help You Grow From Your Pain."[163]

The pandemic, and everything else that 2020 brought with it, forced most people to embrace this simple notion in one way or another. In order to "deal with it," collectively and individually, we first had to accept what it was: a pretty sucky situation—not exactly a reach. I often heard people appreciating little things about the "new normal," whether it was not commuting to work, or having more time for reading, gardening, or family dinners. These simple appreciations demonstrate the power of negative self-help: when you expect the world to suck each day, the bar is pretty low for happiness. And once you've lowered the bar, happiness comes easier.

One way to practice this is through a method called *negative visualization*. It originated with the Cyrenaic philosophers in the fourth century B.C. and was later adopted by Stoic philosophers, including Marcus Aurelius.

Think about what you have in your life, and then imagine your life without them: your significant other, your family, your job, your health, etc. Naturally, you will learn to appreciate what you have, and realize that things maybe aren't as bad as you imagined.

One simple example: Wearing a mask to a local restaurant was a pain; not having that restaurant in your neighborhood would be tragic. If you imagine the impact of that restaurant's closing, suddenly the mask on your face doesn't seem so bad.

The pandemic forced us all to recalibrate.

THINK ABOUT WHAT YOU HAVE IN YOUR LIFE, AND THEN IMAGINE YOUR LIFE WITHOUT THEM: YOUR SIGNIFICANT OTHER, YOUR FAMILY, YOUR JOB, YOUR HEALTH, ETC. NATURALLY, YOU WILL LEARN TO APPRECIATE WHAT YOU HAVE, AND REALIZE THAT THINGS MAYBE AREN'T AS BAD AS YOU IMAGINED.

"GOOD STUFF DOESN'T COME FROM THAT"

In 2014, Dan Harris suffered a panic attack on live TV as a weekend anchor for *Good Morning America*. The experience forced him to reckon with the voice in his head that had been driving him to succeed in a highly competitive business, but also led him down a path of stress and overwhelm. He discovered mindfulness and meditation, and eventually wrote a bestselling book called *10% Happier: How I Tamed the Voice in My Head, Reduced Stress Without Losing My Edge, and Found Self-Help That Actually Works—A True Story*. He followed that up by forming a company and building an app for meditation called 10% Happier; he now hosts a popular podcast with the same name.

When I asked Dan what lesson could be learned from 2020, he pointed to the concept of "productivity shame" from Jocelyn K. Glei, host of the podcast *HurrySlowly*. It's the sense of always feeling behind on our tasks. This leads to beating ourselves up for not getting more accomplished. One way to mitigate this is through self-compassion, the practice of soothing your emotions when things go wrong, or you feel like you're not doing enough.

Dan says he added the practice to his routine in 2020, after years of knowing the research behind it and listening to many of his podcast guests recommend it. The triple hit of the pandemic, the Black Lives Matter movement, and political upheaval propelled Dan, who still anchors ABC's *Nightline* and *Good Morning America* on weekends, to add self-compassion to his regular mediation practice.

"It was a crisis of willingness. But out of desperation, because of all the related stresses from the trio of the pandemic, BLM and politics, and some related to the circumstances of my own life...I was finally willing to do it," Dan told me.[164] "Over time, [I was] seeing that I was really tight in my chest and buried down and trying to bulldoze through, even though I was really tired, and I realized that good stuff doesn't come from that. [Now] I can step away, and put my hand on my chest and—you can make up your own language, but for me it's like 'Dude, you are good. You're making plenty of progress.'"

Dan said he saw a significant increase in podcast downloads (they doubled) and book sales in 2020, a sign that people were looking for help with their mental and emotional health.

If you can be ruthless about prioritization, and practice self-compassion for the items on your list that are not getting done, it will make you happier and more effective.

MAKE COURAGEOUS CONNECTIONS

If you continue to experience stress, anxiety, and symptoms of burnout, you are not alone. Recent studies have found that a majority of American workers are in the same boat. While this is obviously disturbing, it presents an opportunity: you have a license to engage with your colleagues and teammates in new ways.

Amanda Nachman, the author of *#Qualified: You Are More Impressive Than You Realize,* suggests an ambitious plan: Make courageous connections, at least one per day for the next thirty days. It could be someone you know and want to know better, or someone you admire and want to meet.

"Your career journey is not a solo experience," says Amanda.[165] "You are not alone."

Amanda Nachman

She also recommends finding an accountability partner for this exercise. Think of it as being like having a workout partner who motivates you to go the gym because you agreed to meet at a certain time. If you have one person in your life whom you can tell every day whom you connected with, even with a simple text message, it will keep you on track.

I discovered I could use the writing of this book as a license to connect with dozens of people over the past year, some of whom I hadn't spoken with in a very long time. *2020 was a good year for this, since everyone was available!* Neither Amanda nor I, for example, could remember how we originally connected. I had been impressed with her book launch and posts on LinkedIn, so I reached out. We had a great conversation on Zoom and, eventually, I found an email from 2011 describing logistics for the panel discussion at a journalism conference that we were both speaking at—and where we met in person.

If you take nothing else away from this book, I urge you to make more connections with people. Deeper ones, too. Relationships are the key to happiness, in work and in life.

TURN HOPE INTO ACTION

Embracing the suck, facing the despair, and accepting the stumble of 2020 start a process. Once you come to terms with what went wrong, you can begin to see that they can go right again.

"I could easily say 2020 was the worst year of my life by a mile," Gianna says. "And I hope I never have another one like it. I hope our country never has another one like it. But there's a harmonious correction in the universe. I think sometimes that just tilts things on a different axis and makes you take a different perspective. And I don't know if new perspectives are ever a bad thing."

The year 2020 forced everyone to take a different perspective, and gave people a chance to turn hope into action. In early 2021 Gianna told me she has never loved her job more than after the worst year of her life. In writing this book, I've been inspired by so many people who adapted and found new ways to approach their work and life.

One of the most difficult things about a mindset change, or a psychological or emotional tool, is that you have to take it out of the toolbox and use it. You can't just "manifest" it. You have to convert the new idea into a habit and add it to your system. It has to come through action. And 2020 gave people many opportunities to turn hope into action in a way that built the muscle memory to help them in the future.

You didn't think I'd end this book without something positive, did you?

EPILOGUE

"But will the dog eat the dog food?"

—UNKNOWN

This is something investors and venture capitalists have been known to ask when considering whether to invest in a new idea. The question is whether the idea will actually work.

People often ask me how long it took to write this book. As I write this, I can say that I've spent the past twelve months working on this book, in one way or another, almost every day. That's not quite right, however: I've really been working on this book for more than twenty years, and during that time I've tried lots of different kinds of "dog food."

For the ideas and lessons that I have offered in these pages to have any credibility, I think it's important that I can honestly say that I enjoy a certain amount of work-life happiness. And that I've seen positive ripples in my world. As the reader, you'd like to know that I practice what I preach. And that it works.

Life will always be a work in progress, of course. But here's a snapshot of what's going on in my world as I write this:

- I work full time as a management consultant for SmithGeiger, serving the ABC Owned Television Stations. This is my full-time job, with a full stack of Zoom calls and presentations to build on most days.

- I teach two graduate school classes, one called Leadership in Digital Media Economics at the University of North Carolina, and one called Leading Media Enterprises in the Digital Era for Aga Khan University in Kenya, with students from Tanzania and Uganda as well. Yes, both are done remotely. (I use much of the same course material for both.)

- I am a full-time parent to a high school senior, helping to manage the doctors' appointments and prescriptions and mental health challenges of a gender transition, as well as the schoolwork needed to graduate in June and the college application process. My younger son is an art kid who goes to an art school (he designed the butterfly image that is on the cover and used throughout the book), but he needs help with math and physics and the other core classes. He decided last summer to live with me full time, instead of the fifty–fifty parenting plan we had for ten years, to benefit from my structure and systems.

- I'm also helping my twenty-year-old son find his next step in life. He lives with me too, and I regularly offer him exercises to help him find his path, and chores around the house to help him earn money.

- I'm in the process of remodeling an old house I bought a few months ago. I just finished putting in a new floor, new paint and moldings in the basement rec room, and replacing the kitchen faucet. Next, I'm going to replant the backyard and build an outdoor fire pit.

- I'm also in the process of finding a new partner for my life. Those of you in the same boat know how much time it takes for all the swiping, the messaging back and forth, and the first dates that don't lead to second dates.

- I also went skiing twice earlier this week on gorgeous, blue-sky days at Crystal Mountain, where I have been skiing about once a week for months. I always invite friends, who often decline while saying they have too much work and too many family responsibilities to join me. They routinely comment "must be nice" or something similar, partly as a joke, and partly to suggest that I have less on my plate than they do. I love my friends, and know they don't mean any harm; it's just how our culture works.

Soon the weather in the Pacific Northwest will turn, and water skiing and mountain biking will replace snow skiing. I prioritize these seemingly frivolous activities to maintain balance and protect my mental health. This is one of the big rocks in my life that makes all the little rocks work.

How do I have time, given everything else I'm doing? The formula is a combination of many of the things you just read about in this book. I am not suggesting that my life is perfect, or a model to be copied. But I wanted you to know that what I've recommended in the pages of this book has worked for at least one person: me.

Honestly, though, I struggle with guilt from carving time out to feed my mind, body, and soul—especially when that time comes out of normal working hours. I also do much of my work outside of normal working hours, but it's challenging when I know others are doing emails and meetings. Jason Fried and David Heinmeier Hansson call this JOMO—Joy of Missing Out—in their book *It Doesn't Have to be Crazy at Work*. I've long been a fan of how they built Basecamp over the past twenty years with a counterintuitive approach, without goals or working beyond forty hours per week, and I enjoyed their previous book, *ReWork*, as well. But for me, JOMO is still a work in progress. *Maybe it's that good Catholic guilt I grew up with?*

The Butterfly Impact means more than making time to go skiing, of course. It means developing systems that help you be (and feel) productive; prioritize meaning and balance in your life; and devote time and energy to mental and physical health, while developing more connection to the other humans in your world. All of this is in service to those other humans whom you'd like to support and see thrive, whether they are part of your team at work, your friend who needs advice on the weekend, or the teenager who needs help with algebra. I stress daily about the direction and progress of my two sons as they look to start their independent lives, so managing that stress and anxiety is a big part of what I need to accomplish each day.

I can confidently say that, through the process of writing this book, learning from everyone I interviewed and the other research I conducted, I feel better positioned to add value to those around me than ever. I'm more calm, more grounded, more thoughtful, and more grateful than at any other time in my life.

Like the Zen approach to archery or anything else, you identify the goal and then forget about it and concentrate on the process.
—YVON CHOUINARD

Happiness is an accomplishment. And a process. It takes effort and intention, but the rewards are worth it. And the ripples through your world make it that much better.

If you don't think you can do it for you, do it for them.

A MESSAGE
OF THANKS

I owe a great deal of thanks to everyone who spoke with me about this project, and am grateful for all that I've learned on this journey.

This book would not have been possible without the guidance and support of my ad hoc advisory board: Jason Potts, Erin Griffin, Forrest Lindekens, and Hope McCorristin. They barely knew me when we started, but graciously reviewed drafts and joined monthly group Zoom calls, challenging what I wrote or how I presented it. I remember being nervous and pretty anxious for the first call. By the end of the process, I had grown hungry for the feedback and eagerly anticipated the discussion.

Charisse Kiino and Lindsay McGregor gave me confidence in my idea of The Butterfly Impact, even before it was fully formed. They faithfully answered my questions throughout the process and helped me stay the course.

Obviously, the people who shared their stories and experiences, their insights, and their perspectives throughout the book also deserve my thanks. When I first set out to write the book, I did not intend to interview so many people. Each energizing conversation led me to the next one.

I'd also like to thank Christina Verigan at Piper Editorial who helped me with masterful editing in the early phases of the book and Geoff Pope, Caroline Hough, and Ingrid Bartinque from Scribe Media who helped polish the manuscript into its final form. I also want to thank Jordan Christian, Rikki Jump, Skyler White, and the rest of the team at Scribe who made this project better than I ever envisioned.

There are so many other parts to making a book that most people don't see: Liz Driesbach designed a fantastic cover and book jacket; Erinn Hale captured a flattering photo of me; Killer Infographics created, well, killer infographics; and Tracy Goodheart provided me with incredible insights on messaging, social media, and marketing.

There are dozens of other smart people whose names do not appear in the book but were just as instrumental in making this project happen, through thoughtful conversations or in responses to my queries that helped shape my thinking and perspective. Among them are Glenn Thomas, Monica Guzman, Jennifer Mitchell, Anna Robertson, Dave Koste, Steve Rasmussen, Angie Thompson, Lara Zahaba, Wendy Granato, Tom Cibrowski, Bill Taylor, Sarah Gore, Brian Burke, Jodi Wade, Chad Graham, Brian Forth, Sahand Sephernia, John Clark, Elizabeth Osder, Ray Heacox, Steve Brezniak, Jim Rose, Keaton Fuchs, John Kelly, Jessica Hagan, Karren Knowlton, Ann Sobil, Chrissy Petri, Evonne Benedict, Beth Silverberg, Shelia Connolly, Dave Smith, Seth

Geiger, Chris Archer, John Culliton, Nicole Bergen, Michelle Toy, Bill Seitzler, Andrew Finlayson, Cory Bergman, Debra OConnell, John Idler, Lisa Siegel, Britt Guarglia, Sarah Burke, Bernie Prazenica, Cheryl Fair, Michael Carr, Jennifer Graves, Martin Ortiz, Pam Chen, Tracey Watkowski, Bob Monek, John Morris, Jennifer Hoppenstedt, Justin Allen, Rehan Aslam, Courtney Danser, Chad Matthews, Christine Bowley, Olivia Smith, Lisa Clingan-Cruz, Rob Elmore, Emily Sowa, Ricky Courtney, Rachel Schwartz, and Leonard Torres. I can't list everyone who has influenced my thinking over the years but please know that I am grateful for all of my interactions and relationships.

And extra special thanks to my sister, Chrissy Capponi, for locking arms with me a long time ago and joining me on every step of this journey.

I feel enormous gratitude for KEXP and the awesome DJs that programmed the soundtrack for much of my work on this project: John, Cheryl, Kevin, Morgan, Gabriel, Eva, Evie, Abbie, Troy, and the rest have been in my headphones and on my speakers nearly every day since I wrote my first book in 2007. It's an inspiring and supportive community that is driven by many of the same qualities you read about in this book. *And you can stream it online wherever you are in the world at kexp.org.*

Lastly, a special thank you to my parents, Ron and Eileen, for helping me find my way and for always being there for me, through the good times and the bad. Of all the blessings in my life, having amazing parents is at the top of my list.

And thank you for reading. I hope you learned something valuable about resilience, resets, and ripples, and feel better positioned to make a positive impact in the world around you.

ABOUT THE AUTHOR

MARK BRIGGS is the author of three books and a professor of leadership and change management at the University of North Carolina, Chapel Hill. His first book, Journalism 2.0: How to Survive and *Thrive in the Digital Age*, was made available as a free PDF by the Knight Foundation, translated into five languages and downloaded more than 200,000 times. As vice president for SmithGeiger since 2017, he has developed and executed organizational transformation initiatives that have reshaped cultures, helped increase performance, and created more fulfillment among employees. He has traveled to speak and consult in dozens of cities in the US, Europe, China, and the Middle East and spoke at SXSW Interactive in Austin four straight years. He lives in Tacoma, Washington, with his sons Sam and Giallo and can be found most often playing in the mountains or on the water.

Learn more at www.butterfly-impact.com.

NOTES AND REFERENCES

INTRODUCTION

1   Jessica Pryce-Jones calculates that workers will spend an average of 90,000 hours at work in their lifetimes in her book Happiness at Work (Wiley-Blackwell).

2   Bob Chapman comments from Simon Sinek's podcast, *A Bit of Optimism*, June 28, 2020.

3   Kimberly Sakamoto Timoney comments taken from an interview conducted by the author via phone call on June 18, 2020.

CHAPTER 1

4   Taylor Soper, "Airbnb for Child Care: New Seattle Startup Weekdays Wants to Help Parents During Coronavirus Outbreak," *GeekWire*, March 13, 2020, https://www.geekwire.com/2020/airbnb-childcare-new-seattle-startup-weekdays-wants-help-parents-coronavirus-outbreak/.

5   Shauna Causey comments taken from an interview conducted by the author via phone call on November 3, 2020.

6   "Time is money" is an aphorism that originated in "Advice to a Young Tradesman," an essay by Benjamin Franklin that appeared in George Fisher's 1748 book, The American Instructor: or Young Man's Best Companion.

7   Santos from a Yale course titled "The Science of Well-Being," made available through Coursera in March 2020. The research referenced is a combination of two academic papers: "Valuing Time Over Money Is Associated With Greater Happiness," by Ashley V. Whillans, Aaron C. Weidman and Elizabeth W. Dunn, and "People Who Choose Time Over Money Are Happier," by Hal E. Hershfield, Cassie Mogilner, Uri Barnea. Both were published in Social Psychological and Personality Science in 2016.

8   Deepak Chopra, The Ultimate Happiness Prescription: 7 Keys to Joy and Enlightenment, published by Harmony Books, 2009.

9   Franklin Covey, "Big Rocks—Stephen R. Covey" [video], https://resources.franklincovey.com/the-8th-habit/big-rocks-stephen-r-covey.

CHAPTER 2

10   Kellie Garnett comments taken from an interview conducted by the author via email on July 24, 2020.

11   Carol Dweck quote from Mindset: The New Psychology of Success, published by Random House, February 28, 2006.

12   Shawn Achor quote about Fredrickson's research from The Happiness Advantage: The Seven Principles of Positive Psychology That Fuel Success and Performance at Work, published by Currency, September 14, 2010.

13   Nataly Kagan quote from Happier Now: How to Stop Chasing Perfection and Embrace Everyday Moments (Even the Difficult Ones), published by Sounds True Inc., May 1, 2018.

14   Barbara Fredrickson quote from Positivity: Top-Notch Research That Reveals the 3-to-1 Ratio That Will Change Your Life, published by Harmony, December 29, 2009.

CHAPTER 3

15   Mark Mohammadpour comments taken from an interview conducted by the author via video call on August 10, 2020.

16   Chip and Dan Heath's book Switch: How to Change Things When Change is Hard was published by Crown Business, February 16, 2010.

17   Luc de Brabandere's book The Forgotten Half of Change: Achieving Greater Creativity Through Changes in Perception was published by Diversion Books, May 1, 2016.

18   Benjamin Hardy's book Willpower Doesn't Work: Discover the Hidden Keys to Success was published by Hachette Books, March 5, 2019.

CHAPTER 4

19   Derek Sivers quote from the Tim Ferriss Show in December 2015. (Derek says the idea came from Darren Hardy's book *The Compound Effect*.)

20   Paolo Mottola comments taken from an interview conducted by the author via video call on September 25, 2020.

21   Patrick Lencioni, "Make Your Values Mean Something," Harvard Business Review, July 2002, https://hbr.org/2002/07/make-your-values-mean-something.

22   Stephanie Strom, "CVS Vows to Quit Selling Tobacco Products," The New York Times, February 5, 2014, https://www.nytimes.com/2014/02/06/business/cvs-plans-to-end-sales-of-tobacco-products-by-october.html/.

23   Amy Balliett comments taken from an interview conducted by the author via video call on October 6, 2020.

24   Liz Pearce comments taken from an interview conducted by the author via video call on August 6, 2020.

CHAPTER 5

25   Mike Sando comments taken from an interview conducted by the author via phone call on August 26, 2020.

26   Adam Grant's book Originals: How Non-Conformists Move the World was published by Penguin Books, February 7, 2017.

27   Starla Sampaco comments taken from an interview conducted by the author via video call on October 9, 2020.

28   Martin Seligman's book Authentic Happiness: Using the New Positive Psychology to Realize Your Potential for Lasting Fulfillment was published by Atria Books, January 5, 2004.

29   Santos quote from the Yale course "The Science of Well-Being," March 2020.

CHAPTER 6

30   Benjamin Franklin quote has been attributed to others and not directly tied to a specific publication, even though Franklin is the one most widely credited with having first said it.

31   Michelle Li comments taken from an interview conducted by the author via video call on September 30, 2020.

32   Otto comments from "The Exercise Effect: Evidence Is Mounting for the Benefits of Exercise, Yet Psychologists Don't Often Use Exercise as Part of Their Treatment Arsenal. Here's More Research on Why They Should" by Kirsten Weir, December 2011, American Psychological Association. https://www.apa.org/monitor/2011/12/exercise/.

33 Sibold comments from "The 20-Minute Morning Routine Guaranteed to Make Your Day Better: Medications, Meditations, or Chugging Coffee Not Required" by Jeff Haden, Inc.com, December 2013, https://www.inc.com/jeff-haden/20-minutes-guaranteed-to-make-your-whole-day-better-tues.html/.

34 Andrew Solomon's book *The Noonday Demon: An Atlas of Depression* was published by Scribner, 2001.

35 David Allen's book Getting Things Done: The Art of Stress-Free Productivity was published by Penguin Books, December 31, 2002.

36 Liz Pearce comments taken from an interview conducted by the author via video call on August 6, 2020.

37 Bruce Lee's book Wisdom for the Way was published by Black Belt Communications on October 1, 2009. This quote is from podcast No. 63 of the Bruce Lee Podcast series, September 12, 2017, https://brucelee.com/podcast-blog/2017/9/12/63-research-your-own-experience.

38 Paolo Mottola comments taken from an interview conducted by the author via video call on September 25, 2020.

39 Greg McKeown's book Essentialism: The Disciplined Pursuit of Less was published by Currency, April 15, 2014.

40 Marie Kondo and Scott Sonenshein's book Joy at Work: Organizing Your Professional Life was published by Little, Brown Spark, April 7, 2020. Sonenshein's recommendations from his article "How to tidy your to-do list like Marie Kondo" in Fast Company, April 27, 2020, https://www.fastcompany.com/90490780/how-to-tidy-your-to-do-list-the-konmari-way.

41 Tips on how to get started with Getting Things Done from the Critically Most Important Place to Start with GTD, David Allen, March 2, 2020, https://gettingthingsdone.com/2020/03/important-place-to-start-gtd/.

CHAPTER 7

42 Julie Swenson comments taken from an interview conducted by the author via phone call on October 17, 2020.

43 Hal Elrod's book The Miracle Morning: The Not-So-Obvious Secret Guaranteed to Transform Your Life (Before 8AM) was self-published December 7, 2012.

44 "Navy Seal Admiral Shares Reasons to Make Bed Everyday," William H. McRaven, YouTube, posted by Be Better Than Average, January 19, 2015, https://www.youtube.com/watch?v=KgzLzbd-zT4.

45 "Make Your Bed, Change Your Life?" Judy Dutton, *Psychology Today*, August 16, 2012, https://www.psychologytoday.com/us/blog/brain-candy/201208/make-your-bed-change-your-life.

46 Explanation of RAS from "If You Want It, You Might Get It. The Reticular Activating System Explained," Tobias van Schneider, June 22, 2017, https://medium.com/desk-of-van-schneider/if-you-want-it-you-might-get-it-the-reticular-activating-system-explained-761b6ac14e53.

47   Tim Ferriss's book Tools of Titans: The Tactics, Routines, and Habits of Billionaires, Icons, and World-Class Performers was published by Houghton Mifflin Harcourt, December 6, 2016.

48   Atul Gawande's book The Checklist Manifesto: How to Get Things Right was published by Picador, December 1, 2010.

49   Scott Adams' book How to Fail at Almost Everything and Still Win Big: Kind of the Story of My Life was published by Portfolio, October 22, 2013.

CHAPTER 8

50   April Coble comments taken from an interview conducted by the author via phone call on October 12, 2020.

51   April Coble photo courtesy Amos Love.

52   Santos quote from the Yale course "The Science of Well-Being," March 2020.

53   Research by Lavy and Littman-Ovadia and analysis provided by Santos in the Yale course "The Science of Well-Being," March 2020.

54   The $75,000 salary research Santos references in her course came from "High Income Improves Evaluation of Life but Not Emotional Well-Being," a research paper by Daniel Kahneman and Angus Deaton, Center for Health and Well-being, Princeton University, August 4, 2010.

55   Scott Rick comments from "How the Holstee Manifesto Became the New 'Just Do It,'" by Olga Khazan, The Washington Post, November 17, 2011, https://www.washingtonpost.com/business/on-small-business/how-the-holstee-manifesto-became-the-new-just-do-it/2011/11/17/gIQA2AYyUN_story.html/.

56   Mike Radparvar comments taken from an interview conducted by the author via video call on October 23, 2020.

57   Research on negative impacts from hating your job from "This Is What Happens to Your Body When You Hate Your Job," by Monica Torres, Huffington Post, April 17, 2019, https://www.huffpost.com/entry/hate-your-job-body-symptoms_n_5c40a314e4b0a8dbe16e8373. Research cited includes Monique Reynolds from the Center for Anxiety and Behavior Change, E. Kevin Kelloway, the Canada Research Chair in Occupational Health Psychology at St. Mary's University, the American Psychological Association, Harvard University, and Jeffrey Pfeffer's book, Dying for a Paycheck.

58   Jeffrey Pfeffer's book Dying for a Paycheck: How Modern Management Harms Employee Health and Company Performance—and What We Can Do About It was published by Harper Business, March 20, 2018.

59   Adam Davidson's book The Passion Economy: The New Rules for Thriving in the Twenty-First Century was published by Alfred A. Knopf in January 2020.

60   Derek Sivers' book Your Music and People: Creative and Considerate Fame was published by Sound Foundation, January 1, 2020.

61 Warren Buffett's quote from his 1998 speech to The University of Florida's business school as referenced in "Warren Buffett Thinks Working Just to Beef Up Your Résumé is Like 'Saving Up Sex for Your Old Age'" by Myles Udland, Business Insider, November 11, 2015, https://www.businessinsider.com/warren-buffett-on-resume-building-2015-11.

CHAPTER 9

62 McGregor and Doshi's book Primed to Perform: How to Build the Highest Performing Cultures Through the Science of Total Motivation was published by Harper Business, October 6, 2015.

63 Lindsay McGregor comments taken from an interview conducted by the author via phone call on February 3, 2021.

64 Chris Standiford comments taken from an interview conducted by the author via phone call on October 14, 2020.

65 Freshman enrollment figures from "Fit, Culture, Family: How Mark Few and No. 1 Gonzaga Scaled the Mountaintop," by Dana O'Neill, The Athletic, November 25, 2020, https://theathletic.com/2214508/2020/11/25/fit-culture-family-how-mark-few-and-no-1-gonzaga-scaled-the-mountaintop/.

66 Bob Chapman comments from Simon Sinek's podcast, A Bit of Optimism, June 28, 2020.

67 Tanya Andrews comments taken from an interview by the author via email May 17, 2021.

68 "Gamify Your Life and Become Massively Successful," by Deep Patel, Entrepreneur Magazine, March 25, 2019, https://www.entrepreneur.com/article/329405/.

CHAPTER 10

69 Bill Sullivan comments taken from an interview conducted by the author via phone call on September 19, 2020.

70 The Auburn Creed can be found at http://www.auburn.edu/main/welcome/creed.php.

71 Bob Chapman's book Everybody Matters: The Extraordinary Power of Caring for Your People Like Family was published by Portfolio, October 6, 2015.

72 Microsoft buddy system details from "Every New Employee Needs an Onboarding 'Buddy'" by Dawn Klinghoffer, Candice Young, and Dave Haspas, Harvard Business Review, June 6, 2019, https://hbr.org/2019/06/every-new-employee-needs-an-onboarding-buddy.

73 Susan Peppercorn comments from "Starting a New Job? Take Control of Your Onboarding," Harvard Business Review, August 8, 2018, https://hbr.org/2018/08/starting-a-new-job-take-control-of-your-onboarding.

CHAPTER 11

74 DeJuan Hoggard comments taken from an interview conducted by the author via video call on September 15, 2020.

75 Isabel Wilkerson's book Caste: The Origins of Our Discontents was published by Random House, August 4, 2020.

76 Robin DiAngelo's book White Fragility: Why It's So Hard for White People to Talk About Racism was published by Beacon Press, June 26, 2018.

77 The "Women in the Workplace" report was published by LeanIn.org and McKinsey, September 2020, https://www.mckinsey.com/featured-insights/diversity-and-inclusion/women-in-the-workplace.

78 Gender pay disparity research from PayScale's 2020 Annual Salary Survey, https://www.payscale.com/data/gender-pay-gap.

79 Rafat Ali comments from email exchanges and his post on Medium, https://medium.com/@@rafat/the-challenges-in-building-an-inclusive-organization-even-as-a-minority-founder-27c9f037247/.

80 Ruchika Tulshyan comments taken from an interview conducted by the author via phone call on September 15, 2020.

CHAPTER 12

81 Brad Thompson comments taken from an in-person interview conducted by the author on August 13, 2020.

82 Adam Grant's book *Give and Take: A Revolutionary Approach to Success* was published by Weidenfeld & Nicolson, April 11, 2013.

83 Elizabeth Dunn research as referenced in April 2019 TED Talk, "Helping Others Makes Us Happier—but It Matters How We Do It" and in an interview with Professor Laurie Santos as part of the Yale course "Science of Well-Being," March 2020. Her book Happy Money: The Science of Happier Spending was published by Simon & Schuster, May 20, 2014.

84 William Ury comments from his TEDx San Diego talk, "The Power of Listening," January 7, 2015, https://www.youtube.com/watch?v=saXfavo1OQo/.

85 Bob Chapman comments from Simon Sinek's podcast, *A Bit of Optimism*, June 28, 2020.

86 Elaine Helm comments taken from an interview conducted by the author via video call on August 5, 2020.

87 Sigal Barsade comments from "The Ripple Effect: Emotional Contagion and its Influence on Group Behavior," *Administrative Science Quarterly*, 2002, and can be found at https://journals.sagepub.com/doi/abs/10.2307/3094912.

88 Kevin Kelly comments from Freakonomics Radio podcast, May 20, 2020, based on his list of 68 Bits of Unsolicited Advice, which can be found at https://kk.org/thetechnium.

89 Elaine Hatfield quote from Bob Chapman's book *Everybody Matters.*

CHAPTER 13

90 Nicole Thomas comments taken from an interview conducted by the author via phone call on October 15, 2020.

91 Esther Perel's comments from "Relationships at Work with Esther Perel," WorkLife podcast with Adam Grant, March 29, 2020.

92 Tony Schwartz comments from "Why Fear Kills Productivity," The New York Times, December 5, 2014.

93 Liz Pearce comments taken from an interview conducted by the author via video call on August 6, 2020.

94 Patrick Lencioni's book The Five Dysfunctions of a Team: A Leadership Fable was published by Jossey-Bass, April 11, 2002.

95 Frances Frei and Anne Morriss, Unleashed: The Unapologetic Leader's Guide to Empowering Everyone Around You, Harvard Business Review Press, 2020.

96 Frances Frei and Anne Morriss comments from "Begin With Trust: The First Step to Becoming a Genuinely Empowering Leader," Harvard Business Review, May-June 2020. They are also the authors of Unleashed: The Unapologetic Leader's Guide to Empowering Everyone Around You, Harvard Business Review Press, 2020.

97 "Micromoves" from "The Little Things That Affect Our Work Relationships" by Kerry Roberts Gibson and Beth Schinoff, Harvard Business Review, May 29, 2019.

98 Three practices from "How to Mend a Work Relationship" by Brianna Barker Caza, Mara Olekalns, and Timothy J. Vogus, *Harvard Business Review*, February 14, 2020.

CHAPTER 14

99 Sharon Prill comments taken from an interview conducted by the author via video call on September 22, 2020.

100 "Culture eats strategy for breakfast" is a quote frequently attributed to the late management expert Peter Drucker. There is no specific citation for this, however.

101 Tom Davis comments taken from an interview conducted by the author via video call on June 11, 2020.

102 Research on heart attacks from "The Claim: Heart Attacks Are More Common on Mondays," Anahad O'Connor, The New York Times, March 14, 2006.

103 McGregor and Doshi on blame bias from Primed to Perform.

104 Lencioni concept on mining for conflict from The Five Dysfunctions of a Team.

105 Brené Brown quote from her podcast "Dare to Lead: Brené with Kevin Oakes on Cultural Renovation," January 11, 2021.

106 Gallup's 2015 study, "The State of the American Manager," can be found at https://www.gallup.com/ services/182138/state-american-manager.aspx/.

CHAPTER 15

107 Jennifer Sizemore comments taken from an interview conducted by the author via video call on October 12, 2020.

108 Research on how your job can impact your parenting from "Can Your Job Make You a More Controlling Parent?" by Adam Grant, Salon.com, July 15, 2018, https://www.salon.com/2018/07/15/ can-your-job-make-you-a-more-controlling-parent/.

109 Jill Geisler's book Work Happy: What Great Bosses Know was published by Center Street, January 7, 2014.

110 Jill Geisler comments taken from an interview conducted by the author via video call on September 22, 2020.

111 Edgar Schein's book Humble Inquiry: The Gentle Art of Asking Instead of Telling was published by Berrett-Koehler Publishers, September 2, 2013.

112 Marissa Nelson comments taken from an interview conducted by the author via video call on November 8, 2020 and follow-up email correspondence.

113 Mike Stehlik comments taken from an interview conducted by the author via video call on October 13, 2020.

114 Keith Ferrazzi's book Leading Without Authority: How the New Power of Co-Elevation Can Break Down Silos, Transform Teams, and Reinvent Collaboration was published by Currency, May 26, 2020.

115 Fear of communication study by Interact Studio and Harris Poll in 2016 and found in "Two-Thirds of Managers Are Uncomfortable Communicating with Employees" by Lou Solomon, Harvard Business Review, March 9, 2016, https://hbr.org/2016/03/ two-thirds-of-managers-are-uncomfortable-communicating-with-employees.

CHAPTER 16

116 Porsha Grant comments taken from an interview conducted by the author via video call on December 4, 2020.

117 Meg Peters comments taken from an interview conducted by the author via video call on December 11, 2020.

118 Pauline Clance and Suzanne Imes introduced impostor syndrome in "The Impostor Phenomenon in High Achieving Women: Dynamics and Therapeutic Intervention" published in *Psychotherapy: Theory, Research & Practice*, volume 15, 1978, and can be found at http://mpowir.org/wp-content/uploads/2010/02/Download-IP-in-High-Achieving-Women.pdf.

119 "Why Asking for Advice Is More Effective Than Asking for Feedback" by Jaewon Yoon, Hayley Blunden, Ariella Kristal, and Ashley Whillans was published by *Harvard Business Review*, September 20, 2019, and can be found at https://hbr.org/2019/09/why-asking-for-advice-is-more-effective-than-asking-for-feedback.

120 Adam Grant comments from "How to Love Criticism" by Adam Grant, WorkLife podcast, March 2018.

121 Dave Smith comment taken from a phone call with the author in June 2017.

CHAPTER 17

122 Jen Lee Reeves comments taken from an interview conducted by the author via video call on September 24, 2020.

123 "Columbia Teen Included as Finalist for TIME's Kid of the Year" by Stephanie Southey, Columbia Missourian, Dec. 3, 2020, https://www.columbiamissourian.com/news/local/columbia-teen-included-as-finalist-for-times-kid-of-the-year/article_9ad2a528-9e9a-50c4-a8c0-89555dc49477.html.

124 Andrew Tarvin's book Humor That Works: The Missing Skill for Success and Happiness at Work was published by Page Two, April 1, 2019. Example jokes from "101 Funny Work Jokes to Get You Through the Day," https://www.humorthatworks.com/database/funny-work-jokes-to-get-you-through-the-day/.

125 Wendy McMahon comments taken from an interview conducted by the author via email on September 4, 2020.

126 Sophie Scott comment and Bruce Daisley comments from "Laughter Is the Sign of a Strong Team—and a Trustworthy Leader" by Bruce Daisley, Business Insider, February 25, 2020, https://www.businessinsider.com/former-twitter-vp-laughter-sign-strong-team-trustworthy-leader-2020-2.

127 Mayo Clinic information from "Stress Relief from Laughter? It's No Joke" by Mayo Clinic staff, April 5, 2019, https://www.mayoclinic.org/healthy-lifestyle/stress-management/in-depth/stress-relief/art-20044456.

128 Study on jokes in presentations from "Sarcasm, Self-Deprecation, and Inside Jokes: A User's Guide to Humor at Work," by Brad Bitterly and Alison Wood Brooks, Harvard Business Review, July–August 2020, https://hbr.org/2020/07/sarcasm-self-deprecation-and-inside-jokes-a-users-guide-to-humor-at-work.

CHAPTER 18

129 T'wina Nobles comments taken from an interview conducted by the author via phone call on December 8, 2020.

130 "How Gratitude Can Transform Your Workplace" by Kira M. Newman, Greater
Good Magazine, September 6, 2017, https://greatergood.berkeley.edu/article/item/
how_gratitude_can_transform_your_workplace.

131 "The Former CEO of Campbell Soup Sent 30,000 Handwritten Thank-you Notes to Employees—Here's
Why it's a Great Leadership Strategy" by Shana Lebowitz, Business Insider Australia, September 2, 2016,
https://www.businessinsider.com.au/why-leaders-should-show-gratitude-to-their-employees-2016-9.

132 Blake Mycoskie's book Start Something That Matters was published by Random House, May 15, 2002.

133 "On the Relationship of Hope and Gratitude to Corporate Social Responsibility" by Lynne Andersson,
Temple University; Robert A. Giacalone, John Carroll University; Carole L. Jurkiewicz, University of
Colorado Colorado Springs, Journal of Business Ethics, February 2007.

134 "31 Benefits of Gratitude: The Ultimate Science-Backed Guide," Happier Human, https://www.
happierhuman.com/the-science-of-gratitude.

CHAPTER 19

135 Lynn Edwards comments taken from an interview conducted by the author via phone call on Dec. 11,
2020.

136 "Conferences After Covid Will Be Shorter—and Smarter," by Joanna Pearlstein, Wired.com, December 14,
2020, https://www.wired.com/story/what-conferences-will-look-like-post-covid.

137 "Don't Waste a Good Crisis" originally appeared in 1976 according to Freakonomics
by Stephen Dubner and Steven Leavitt, https://freakonomics.com/2009/08/13/
quotes-uncovered-who-said-no-crisis-should-go-to-waste.

138 John F. Kennedy quote from his speech at the convocation of the United Negro College Fund,
Indianapolis, Indiana, April 12, 1959.

139 Bear Bryant quote from "100 Years of Bear Bryant; 100 Facts You May Not Know" by Jon Solomon,
AL.com, September 11, 2013.

140 Brad Benson comments taken from an interview conducted by the author via phone call on January 10,
2020.

141 Findings are from an online poll conducted by OptionB.Org and SurveyMonkey November 6-7, 2020.
The sample consists of 2,050 US adults age eighteen or over. More details are available at https://optionb.
org/optionbthere/holiday-survey-results-2020.

142 Family dinner research from the Guelph Family Health Study cited by the Family Dinner Project in its
September 2020 newsletter which can be found at https://thefamilydinnerproject.org/?p=26776.

143 "Black Lives Matter May Be the Largest Movement in US History" by Larry Buchanan, Quoctrung Bui,
and Jugal K. Patel, The New York Times, July 3, 2020, https://www.nytimes.com/interactive/2020/07/03/
us/george-floyd-protests-crowd-size.html.

144 10,600 BLM protest events in the United States and 93 percent peaceful according to research by Armed Conflict Location & Event Data Project (ACLED), https://acleddata.com/2020/09/03/demonstrations-political-violence-in-america-new-data-for-summer-2020.

145 "President-Elect Joe Biden Hits 80 Million Votes In Year Of Record Turnout" by Domenico Montanaro, NPR, November 25, 2020, https://www.npr.org/2020/11/25/937248659/president-elect-biden-hits-80-million-votes-in-year-of-record-turnout.

CHAPTER 20

146 James Doty's book *Into the Magic Shop: A Neurosurgeon's Quest to Discover the Mysteries of the Brain and the Secrets of the Heart* was published by Avery, February 2, 2016.

147 Joe Hurd comments taken from an interview conducted by the author via video call on December 7, 2020.

148 Rob Acker comments taken from an interview conducted by the author via phone call on August 12, 2020.

149 Elizabeth Gilbert quote from How to Live a Good Life by Jonathan Fields, Hay House Books, 2016.

150 Gianna Biscontini comments taken from an interview conducted by the author via video call on January 20, 2021.

151 "Life Lessons from 2020" by Mark Manson, https://markmanson.net/life-lessons-from-2020.

152 Bill Gates comment and research on the effects of business travel from "Flying Isn't All that Necessary: Grounded Business Execs Express Relief at Suspension of Non-stop Travel" by Suzanne Bearne, Digiday, January 12, 2021, https://digiday.com/media/grounded-business-execs-express-relief/.

CHAPTER 21

153 Shasta Nelson comments taken from an interview conducted by the author via video call on January 5, 2021.

154 Scott Berkun's book *The Year Without Pants: WordPress.com and the Future of Work* was published by Jossey-Bass, September 10, 2013.

155 "Distributed Work's Five Levels of Autonomy" by Matt Mullenweg, April 10, 2020, https://ma.tt/2020/04/five-levels-of-autonomy/.

156 Matt Mullenweg comments from Sam Harris podcast, *Making Sense*, episode #194: "The New Future of Work," March 24, 2020. https://samharris.org/podcasts/194-new-future-work/.

157 Matt Thompson comments taken from an interview conducted by the author via video call on January 26, 2021.

158 "Take Your Lunch Break!" by Ruchika Tulshyan, Harvard Business Review, January 21, 2021, https://hbr.org/2021/01/take-your-lunch-break.

CHAPTER 22

159 Jennifer Deger comments taken from an interview conducted by the author via phone call on December 21, 2020.

160 Gianna Biscontini comments taken from an interview conducted by the author via video call on January 20, 2021.

161 Oliver Burkeman's book The Antidote: Happiness for People Who Can't Stand Positive Thinking was published by Farrar, Straus and Giroux, November 5, 2013.

162 "Toxic Positivity: The Dark Side of Positive Vibes" by Samara Quintero, LMFT, CHT and Jamie Long, PsyD., The Psychology Group, https://thepsychologygroup.com/toxic-positivity/.

163 "6 Books that Will Help You Grow from Your Pain" by Mark Manson, https://markmanson.net/6-books-to-grow-from-your-pain. (Also worth a read are Mark Manson's "5 Tenets of Negative Self-Help," https://markmanson.net/negative-self-help.)

164 Dan Harris comments taken from an interview conducted by the author via video call on February 2, 2021.

165 Amanda Nachman's book #Qualified: You Are More Impressive Than You Realize was published by Lifestyle Entrepreneurs Press, September 1, 2020.